AuthorHouse™ UK Ltd.
500 Avebury Boulevard
Central Milton Keynes, MK9 2BE
www.authorhouse.co.uk
Phone: 08001974150

First published by AuthorHouse 7/29/2009

ISBN: 978-1-4389-9319-5 (sc)

This book is printed on acid-free paper.

The Core Aspects of International Financial Reporting Standards and International Accounting Standards

by

Steve Collings
Leavitt Walmsley Associates

in association with
AccountancyStudents.co.uk

Preface

This publication has been written as a reference guide to the core technical aspects contained within the International Financial Reporting Standards (IFRS) and the International Accounting Standards (IAS). Some IFRS and IAS are extremely complicated and can often cause a lot of ambiguity for preparers of financial statements reporting under the IFRS framework. This publication is also intended as a revision aid for students who are studying for their professional accountancy examinations.

This publication is intended to be a reference guide to the mainstream International Financial Reporting Standards and the International Accounting Standards for student revision but not as a substitute for study material. It is also intended to be used by preparer's of financial statements using IFRS as a reference guide to the core contents of each IFRS/IAS. This publication is not a substitute for the mainstream standards which should always be consulted in the event of ambiguity.

The author, publisher, AccountancyStudents.co.uk nor Leavitt Walmsley Associates cannot be held responsible for any loss arising from reliance on this publication. The author recommends this guidance is used as is intended, being that of a study-aid or reference material.

Any errors in this publication are the author's own and come with his apologies.

Acknowledgements

My thanks and gratitude go to all my friends, family and colleagues who have supported mc over the years and helped me to achieve my goals to do what I do best – in particular Les Leavitt from LWA. I would also like to extend my thanks to all my colleagues on AccountancyStudents.co.uk, particularly Annette Smyth and Mark Ellis, for the help and support over the years and extend my thanks to the publisher.

The Author

Steve Collings FMAAT ACCA DipIFRS started his career working in industry. In 1998 he decided to leave industry and pursue his career in practice. Steve qualified as an AAT in 2000 and then went on to qualify as an ACCA in 2005. Steve also holds the ACCA's Diploma in International Financial Reporting Standards.

Steve works as Audit and Technical Manager at Leavitt Walmsley Associates Chartered Certified Accountants who are based in Manchester specialising in auditing and financial reporting as well as having an interest in small business taxation. Steve trained and qualified with the firm. In addition, Steve is also a partner in AccountancyStudents.co.uk and lectures student accountants on financial reporting issues.

Steve has published several articles in the various accounting media on auditing, financial reporting and small business taxation issues for both students and qualified accountants.

The Framework

The objective of the Framework Document is to set out the concepts that underlie the preparation and presentation of financial statements for external users as set out in the *'Framework for the Preparation and Presentation of Financial Statements'*. It is important at the outset to understand that the Framework Document itself is not a standard – its primary purpose is to assist the IASB in developing new or revised accounting standards and to assist preparers of financial statements applying accounting standards and dealing with issues which are not covered by accounting standards.

It covers:

- the objectives;
- the underlying assumptions;
- the qualitative characteristics;
- the elements of financial statements; and
- the concepts of capital and capital maintenance.

THE OBJECTIVES

The objective of financial statements is to provide information about:

- the financial position;
- the financial performance; and
- changes in financial position

of a reporting entity that is useful to a wide range of users in making economic decisions. If we consider how the above are reported within the financial statements:

The *financial position* = the statement of financial position (previously the balance sheet)

The *financial performance* = the statement of comprehensive income (previously the income statement)

The *changes in financial position* = the statement of cash flows (previously the cash flow statement)

The Financial Position

The financial position of an entity is affected by:

(a) the economic resources under its control;
(b) the way it is financially structured;
(c) the entity's liquidity and solvency; and
(d) the entity's capacity to adapt to change.

The Financial Performance

The financial performance (primarily profitability) can be assessed to:

(a) predict the opportunity to generate cash flows from the resources the entity controls; and
(b) to form judgements above how the resources employed by the entity are effective.

Changes in Financial Position

These can be used to assess the investing, financing and operating activities as well as evaluating the entity's ability to generate cash and cash equivalents. In addition to evaluating the entity's ability to generate cash and cash equivalents, the changes in financial position can also be assessed to see how the entity uses those cash flows. The statement of cash flows is useful because it can convey information to the user of the financial statements which might not otherwise be conveyed in the statement of comprehensive income or the statement of financial position. A typical example is the amount of taxation *paid* during the year.

THE UNDERLYING ASSUMPTIONS

There are two fundamental terms which you will come across in the Framework:

(a) the accruals basis of accounting; and
(b) the going concern basis.

The Accruals Basis

The accruals basis of accounting stipulates that an entity should recognise the effects of transactions and other events when they occur and not when they are paid or when cash is received in settlement.

In addition, an entity should also recognise these transactions and events in the financial statements in the period to which they relate. Consider the following example:

Ian Lucas Security Shutters Inc has a reporting date of 31 December. It receives a rent demand on 15 December for the period 1 January to 31 March. If Ian Lucas Security Shutters were to include this rent demand in its financial statements to 31 December, then this would distort the financial statements. The reason the financial statements would be distorted is because the period the rent demand relates to falls within the next financial year (1 January to 31 March). If it includes this invoice within the accounting system, then a prepayment of the full amount of the rent demand should be made to carry forward the demand to the next reporting period.

Conversely, if the rent demand related to 1 October to 31 December but was received on 10 January then the financial statements should include this amount as it relates to the financial year in question.

By complying with the accruals concept this ensures that the financial statements inform users of obligations to pay cash in the future and also inform users of the entity's obligations to also receive cash in the future.

The Going Concern Basis

If financial statements are prepared on a going concern basis, this assumes that the entity will continue in operation for the foreseeable future. This informs the user that the entity neither intends to liquidate or materially curtail the scale of operations.

The Qualitative Characteristics

There are four qualitative characteristics which the IASB's Framework Document refers to. They are:

(a) understandability;
(b) comparability;
(c) relevance; and
(d) reliability

Understandability and comparability are both 'presentation' issues within a set of financial statements. Relevance and reliability are both 'content' issues.

Understandability

Users of financial statements are assumed to have a good understanding of the business which the financial statements relate to as well as its activities. The users are expected to have a knowledge of financial issues, and information about complicated matters should not be excluded on the basis that the entity considers the information to be too complicated for the users to understand.

Comparability

Users of financial statements must be able to compare financial statements of an entity to different entities in order to evaluate the financial position, performance and changes in financial position.

In addition, users should also be able to compare the financial statements of an entity through time, for example from one year to the next, therefore financial statements must show corresponding information for preceding periods (these are often referred to as 'comparatives').

If an entity changes an accounting policy this is the reason why a prior year adjustment needs to be undertaken in order to aid comparability. This ensures consistent measurement and display of the financial effect of like transactions and other events.

Relevance

Information must be relevant in both nature and materiality. Information is material if its omission or misstatement could influence the economic decisions of users taken on the basis of the financial statements. Relevance could also be determined by nature alone. Consider this example:

> Stella Inc sold Janet Inc some goods amounting to $100,000. Stella Inc also has a controlling interest in Janet Inc. The sale of goods from Stella to Janet is one piece of information. The fact that Stella Inc has a controlling interest in Janet Inc is dealt with in IAS 24 'Related Party Disclosures'.

Reliability

For financial statements to be reliable they need to be free from material error and bias. In addition, they should demonstrate faithful representation, prudence and completeness. Completeness should be within the margins of both cost and materiality but taking into consideration that an omission could cause information to be false or misleading resulting in unreliability. An item is 'material' if its error or omission could affect the decisions made by the user of the financial statements.

Transactions within a set of financial statements should relate to their 'substance' rather than their legal form. This is particularly important when it comes to deciphering the treatment of leases (IAS 17 'Leases'), goods on consignment (IAS 18 'Revenue') and financial instruments (IAS 39 'Financial Instruments: Recognition and Measurement'). The concept of 'prudence' does still exist, though is very much subordinate to that of 'substance'.

The Elements of the Financial Statements

Financial statements are made up of the following elements:

   (a) assets;
   (b) liabilities;
   (c) equity;
   (d) income; and;
   (e) expenses

Assets

An asset is a resource controlled by the entity as a result of past events from which future economic benefits are expected to flow.

Remember, 'control' means the ability to restrict the use of the asset – for example inventory could be stored in a locked warehouse. In contrast, if an entity has a highly skilled workforce then it cannot recognise these as an asset because the entity cannot 'control' its workforce – they could leave at any time.

Liabilities

A liability is a present obligation of the entity arising from past events, settlement of which is expected to result in an outflow of resources embodying economic benefits.

Illustration

Leyla Enterprises Inc have an item of plant that requires a routine overhaul every five years. The Directors of Leyla Enterprises Inc wish to provide for $1/5^{th}$ of the cost of the future overhauls.

Solution

The Directors cannot provide for the future overhaul costs. These costs are merely an 'intention' at the reporting date as opposed to an 'obligation'. The Directors could well sell the item of plant before the five years has expired.

Equity

Equity is the residual interest in the assets of the entity after deducting all its liabilities.

Income

Income is increases in economic benefits during the reporting period in the form of inflows (or enhancements) of assets or decreases of liabilities that result in increases in equity other than those relating to contributions from equity participants.

Income can include revenue and gains even though they may be included in equity rather than the statement of comprehensive income (for example a revaluation surplus).

An example of a contribution from equity participants is the purchase of additional shares.

Expenses

Expenses are decreases in economic benefits during the reporting period in the form of outflows (or depletions) of assets or incurrences of liabilities that result in decreases in equity other than those relating to distributions to equity participants.

Capital and Capital Maintenance

There are two concepts of 'capital'. There is the 'financial' concept and there is the 'physical' concept.

Financial Concept

The financial concept of capital is the same as net assets or equity of the entity.

It works on the basis that profit is earned only if the financial amount of the net assets at the end of the period is more than the financial amount of net assets at the beginning of the period after excluding any distributions to, or contributions from, the owners during the period.

Physical Concept

The physical concept is regarded as the productive capacity of the entity based on operating capability.

It works on the basis that profit is earned only if the physical productive capacity of the entity at the end of the period is in excess of the physical productive capacity at the beginning of the period after excluding any distributions to, or contributions from, the owners during the period.

IFRS 1
First-Time Adoption of IFRS

OBJECTIVE

The objective of IFRS 1 is to make sure that a reporting entity who adopts IFRS as its financial reporting basis prepares financial statements that:

- are clear for users and achieve 'comparability' over all the periods presented within the financial statements;

- provide a suitable starting point for reporting under IFRS; and

- can be generated at a cost that does not exceed benefits to users.

An entity who chooses IFRS as its financial reporting basis must prepare an opening balance sheet (statement of financial position) at the date of transition to IFRS. In preparing its opening balance sheet (statement of financial position), a reporting entity must;

(a) recognise all IFRS assets and liabilities
(b) not recognise assets and liabilities not permitted by IFRS
(c) classify assets and liabilities by IFRS
(d) apply IFRS in measuring all recognised assets and liabilities

---

Illustration

Alex Inc has a year end of 31 December 2008 and has decided to report under IFRS.

Required

What is the 'transition date' for the opening balance sheet (statement of financial position) that Alex Inc will have to prepare under the principles of IFRS 1?

Solution

The 'transition date' is the start of the earliest period for which comparative information is provided. Therefore as 2007 is the comparative year, the start of this period is 1 January 2007 (i.e. the closing 2006 trial balance).

Exemptions

IFRS 1 grants limited exemptions in certain areas where the costs of complying with the requirements would outweigh the benefits to the users of financial statements.

IFRS 2
Share-Based Payment

OBJECTIVE

The objective of this standard is to outline the financial reporting requirements that an entity who engages in share-based payment transactions should comply with in their financial statements. It outlines the requirements an entity is to reflect in both its profit and loss account (statement of comprehensive income) and its balance sheet (statement of financial position) that the effects of share-based payments has on the entity's financial statements.

IFRS 2 covers three types of share-based payment transactions:

- Equity-settled share-based payment transactions where the entity receives goods or services as consideration for equity instruments of the entity, including shares or share options.

- Cash-settled share-based payment transactions where the entity acquires goods or services by incurring liabilities to the supplier of those goods or services for amounts which are based on the price or value of the entity's shares or other equity instruments of the entity.

- Transactions in which the entity receives or acquires goods or services and the terms of the arrangement provide either the entity or the supplier of those goods or services with a choice of whether the entity settles the transaction in either cash or by issuing equity instruments.

Where an entity has equity-settled share-based payment transactions, an entity should measure the goods or services received together with any corresponding increase in equity, directly at the fair value of the goods or services received. Where the fair value cannot be reliably estimated, then the entity is required to measure their value, together with the corresponding increase in equity, indirectly by reference to the fair value of the equity instruments granted.

IFRS 2 also states that:

- Transactions with employees and third parties providing similar services should be measured at the fair value of the equity instruments granted at the grant date.

- Transactions with parties other than employees have a rebuttable presumption (which is rarely rebutted) that the fair value of the goods or services received can be reliably estimated. The fair value is measured at the date the entity receives the goods or services.

- Where goods or services are measured at fair value of the equity instruments granted, IFRS 2 specifies that vesting conditions, other than market conditions, are NOT taken into account when estimating the fair values of the shares or options at the measurement date. Vesting conditions are taken into account by adjusting the number of equity instruments included in the measurement of the transaction.

- IFRS 2 requires fair values are to be based on market prices, where these are available. Where market prices are not available, then fair value is estimated by using a valuation technique to arrive at a valuation that estimates what the value of the equity instruments would be at the measurement date in an arm's length transaction with knowledgeable and willing persons.

Where cash-settled share-based payments are made, these must be measured by the entity at the fair value of the liability. An entity is also required under the provisions of IFRS 2 to remeasure the fair value of the liability at each reporting date until the liability is settled.

Where an entity enters into a share-based payment transaction where the terms of the arrangement allow the entity to settle the transaction in cash or equity instruments, then the entity should account for these as a cash-settled share-based payment transaction.

Illustration

Lucas Inc grants two thousand share options to each of its 3 directors on 1 January 2008. The terms of the option are that the directors must still be in the employment of Lucas Inc on 31 December 2010 when the options vest. The fair value of each option as at 1 January 2008 is $10 and all of the options are expected to vest. The options will only vest if Lucas Inc share price reaches $16 per share. As at 31 December 2008, the share price was only $7 per share and it is not expected to rise in the next two years. Further, it is expected that only two directors will be employed as at 31 December 2010.

Required

Show how the share options will be treated in the financial statements of Lucas Inc for the year ended 31 December 2008.

Solution

The increase in the share price should be ignored for the purposes of calculating the value of the share options as at 31 December 2008. The fact that only two directors will be employed as at 31 December 2010 must, however, be taken into account, therefore:

2,000 options x 2 directors x $10 x 1 year / 3 years = $13,333.

The journals required are:

DR   income statement (statement of comprehensive income)
        CR   equity balance sheet (statement of financial position)

IFRS 3
Business Combinations

OBJECTIVE

The objective of this IFRS is to deal with the information that an entity provides within their financial statements about a business combination and the effect that this combination has on the reporting entity's financial statements. IFRS 3 deals with how an acquirer:

- recognises and measures in its financial statements the identifiable assets acquired, the liabilities assumed and any non-controlling interest in the acquiree;
- recognises and measures the goodwill acquired in the business combination or a gain from a bargain purchase; and
- determines what information to disclose to enable users of the financial statements to evaluate the nature and financial effects of the business combination.

The 'Acquisition Method' of Accounting

When a business acquires another business, the business combination must be accounted for by applying the 'acquisition method' of accounting. Essentially, one party in the transaction is the 'acquirer' and the entity that is being acquired is the 'acquiree'.

All identifiable assets and liabilities of the acquiree are measured at their acquisition-date fair value. Any non-controlling interest in an acquiree is measured at fair value or as the non-controlling interest's proportionate share of the acquiree's net identifiable assets. (Note – 'non-controlling interest' was previously known as 'minority interest' before the revisions to IFRS 3). The non-controlling interest is the interest held in the equity shares of the acquiree by outside investors.

The IFRS requires an acquirer to identify any difference between:

- the aggregate of the consideration transferred, any non-controlling interest in the acquiree and (in the case of step acquisitions) the acquisition-date fair value of the acquirer's previously held equity interest in the acquiree; and
- the net identifiable assets acquired.

The difference between the two will generally be recognised as goodwill. In the situation where there is a bargain purchase then the gain will instead be recognised in the statement of comprehensive income. Any consideration (including contingent consideration) is measured at fair value.

Disclosure Requirements

IFRS 3 requires the acquirer to disclose information within the financial statements that enables the user of the financial statements to evaluate the nature and financial effect of the business combination(s) that occurred during the reporting period, or a period after the reporting date but before the financial statements are authorised for issue. After a business combination, the acquirer must also disclose any adjustments recognised in the current reporting period that relate to business combinations that occurred in the current or previous reporting periods.

Recent Amendments to IFRS 3

There have been some major amendments to IFRS 3 which occurred in January 2008. The main reason for the changes in IFRS 3 were so that the standard itself was more fully converged with US GAAP and to place greater emphasis on control. A summary of the major changes are as follows:

Goodwill

Goodwill can be recognised in full even where control is less than 100%. Before the revisions to IFRS 3, the IFRS stated that on acquisition, goodwill should only be recognised with respect to the part of the subsidiary undertaking that is attributable to the interest held by the parent. This is still an option in IFRS 3 but now goodwill can be recognised in full which now means that the non-controlling interest will be measured at fair value and be included within goodwill.

Illustration

Alicia Enterprises Inc purchases an 80% equity stake in Alex Inc for $100. The net assets of Alex Inc at the date of acquisition were $50.

Required

Calculate the goodwill to be recognised in Alicia Inc financial statements using the 'old' method and the 'revised' method of goodwill recognition.

Solution

Using the 'old' method of goodwill recognition, goodwill will be calculated as follows:

	$
Cost of investment	100
Net assets acquired: ($50 x 80%)	(40)
Goodwill to be recognised	60

Under the 'revised' method, the non-controlling interest goodwill is measured at fair value in order to include their share of the goodwill. If we estimate that the fair value of the non-controlling interests share of goodwill is $10, then the calculation is as follows:

	$
Cost of investment	100
Net assets acquired: ($50 x 80%)	(40)
	60
Non-controlling interest share of goodwill	10
Goodwill under the 'revised' method	70

The non-controlling interest share of the goodwill is included in Alicia Inc's statement of financial position (balance sheet) as follows:

DR Goodwill (non-current assets)
  CR   non-controlling interests (equity section)

Acquisition-Related Costs

Previously transaction costs associated with a business combination (for example legal fees and accountancy fees for due diligence work) were capitalised along with the cost of the acquisition thus forming part of the goodwill calculation. The IASB have concluded that these types of cost must now be expensed as these costs are not part of the fair value exchange between the buyer and seller of the business. This means, therefore, that in the year of acquisition, the acquirer's income statement will show substantially higher legal and professional fees. However, this reduction in profits should be outweighed in future years because the annual impairment test on the goodwill will be based on a reduced initial balance.

Step Acquisitions

Prior to the revisions of IFRS 3, it was a requirement to measure the assets and liabilities at fair value at every step of the transaction to calculate a 'portion' of goodwill. This requirement was removed during the revision process. Instead you should measure goodwill as the difference, at the acquisition date, between the fair value of any interest in the business held before the acquisition, the consideration transferred and the net assets acquired.

Partial Acquisitions

Non-controlling interests are measured as their proportionate interest in the net identifiable assets (as was the case before IFRS 3 was revised). Non-controlling interests can also be measured at fair value.

Recognition of Assets and Liabilities Subject to Contingencies

There were a few (limited) changes to the assets and liabilities recognition under IFRS 3. There is a new requirement to recognise assets and liabilities that are subject to contingencies at fair value at the acquisition date. Any subsequent changes in fair value will be accounted for in accordance with other IFRS's (which will usually be in profit or loss) rather than as an adjustment to goodwill.

Partial Disposal of a Subsidiary Whilst Control is Retained

Where a partial disposal of an investment in a subsidiary is disposed of whilst control is retained, then this is accounted for as an equity transaction with owners and a gain or loss is not recognised.

A partial disposal of an interest in a subsidiary where the parent loses control, but retains an interest and thus becomes (for example) an associate, will trigger recognition of a gain or loss on the entire interest. A realised gain or loss is recognised on the portion that has been disposed of; a holding gain is recognised on the interest retained, calculated as the difference between the fair value and book value of the retained interest.

Acquisition of Shares after Control has been Obtained

Where the parent acquires some, or all of, the non-controlling interest in a subsidiary, then this should be treated as a treasury share-type transaction and therefore should be accounted for as an equity transaction. There is an interpretation summary, IFRIC 11 *'IFRS 2: Group and Treasury Share Transactions'* which gives guidance in this area.

IFRS 4
Insurance Contracts

OBJECTIVE

The objective of this IFRS is to deal with the financial reporting for insurance contracts by an entity that issues insurance contracts (for example an insurance company to its policyholders).

An insurance contract is defined as a contract under which one party (the insurer) accepts significant insurance risk from another party (i.e. the policyholder) by agreeing to compensate the policyholder if a specific uncertain future event (the insured event) adversely affects the policyholder.

IFRS 4 applies to all insurance contracts that an entity issues and to reinsurance contracts that it holds, except for certain contracts that are dealt with in other IFRS's such as IAS 39 *Financial Instruments: Recognition and measurement*.

IFRS 4 also contains the following provisions which entities involved in insurance contracts must comply with. Specifically, IFRS 4:

- prohibits provisions for potential claims under contracts that do not exist at the end of the reporting period;

- requires a test for the adequacy of recognised insurance liabilities and requires an impairment test to be carried out for reinsurance assets; and

- requires an insurer to keep insurance liabilities in its statement of financial position (balance sheet) until such time that they are discharged, cancelled or expire. It also requires an entity to present insurance liabilities without offsetting them against related reinsurance assets.

An entity who has to report using IFRS 4 can change its accounting policies for insurance contracts but only, if as a result, the financial statements present information that is more relevant and no less reliable, or more reliable and no less relevant. The IFRS also stipulates that an insurer cannot:

- measure insurance liabilities on an undiscounted basis;

- measure contractual rights to future investment management fees at an amount that exceeds their fair value by comparison with current fees charged by other market participants for similar services; and

- use non-uniform accounting policies for the insurance liabilities of subsidiaries.

IFRS 5
Non-Current Assets Held for Sale and Discontinued Operations

OBJECTIVE

The objective of IFRS 5 is to specify how assets that both qualify for, and are treated as, 'held for sale' should be presented and disclosed within a set of financial statements. The standard also deals with discontinued operations.

A non-current asset (or disposal group) that is held for sale must be up for sale in its present condition and the sale must be highly probable. In order for the sale to be classed as 'highly probable', there must be certain characteristics present. These are as follows:

- management must be committed to a plan to sell the asset;

- there must be an active programme of seeking a buyer;

- the asset (or disposal group) must be available for immediate sale;

- the sale is highly probable; and

- the sale is expected to complete within one year of the asset being classified as held for sale.

Where an asset (or disposal group) is classified as 'held for sale' then depreciation of such an asset or disposal group must cease as soon as it is classified as 'held for sale'. The asset (or disposal group) should be carried in the statement of financial position (balance sheet) at the *lower* of the carrying amount in the statement of financial position (balance sheet) and fair value less costs to sell. 'Fair value' is essentially how much could be received by knowledgeable and willing persons in exchange for the asset in an arm's length transaction.

Discontinued Operations

A discontinued operation is a part of an entity that has either been disposed of or is classified as held for sale (e.g. a division of a manufacturing plant). A discontinued operation should:

- represent a separate major line of business or geographical area of operations;

- be part of a single co-ordinated plan to dispose of a separate major line of business or geographical area of operation; or

- be a subsidiary acquired exclusively with a view to resale.

Where an entity has a discontinued operation, that component of the entity's operations and cash flows must be clearly distinguished both operationally and for financial reporting purposes from the rest of the entity.

For financial reporting purposes, the revenue, expenses, pre-tax profit or loss and the income tax expense of the discontinued operation should be separately presented on the face of the statement of comprehensive income (income statement) or in the notes to the financial statements.

IFRS 6
Exploration for and Evaluation of Mineral Resources

OBJECTIVE

The objective of this IFRS is to deal with the financial reporting requirements for entities who operate in the mineral extractive industry.

Exploration for and evaluation of mineral resources is the search for mineral resources (e.g. oil or natural gas) after the entity has obtained legal rights to explore in a specific area.

In summary, IFRS 6 permits an entity to develop an accounting policy for exploration and evaluation assets without specifically considering the requirements of paragraphs 11 and 12 of IAS 8 *Accounting Policies, Changes in Accounting Estimates and Errors*. As a result of this requirement in IFRS 6 an entity can still continue to use the accounting policies it adopted immediately before adopting IFRS (for example a company who previously reported under UK GAAP).

Where circumstances change which may give rise to the carrying amount of the exploration and evaluation assets being in excess of recoverable amount, then IFRS 6 requires an impairment test to be undertaken. The actual recognition of impairment does vary in IFRS 6 but once impairment has been identified, then IFRS 6 requires the entity to measure the impairment in accordance with the provisions laid down in IAS 36 *Impairment of Assets*.

The IFRS also requires that an entity determine an accounting policy for allocation of exploration and evaluation assets to cash-generating units or groups of cash-generating units for the purposes of impairment testing.

IFRS 7
Financial Instruments: Disclosures

OBJECTIVE

This is a relatively new IFRS which came into force for annual periods beginning on or after 1 January 2007, with earlier adoption permitted. Its objective is to deal with the disclosures required in an entity's financial statements in connection with financial instruments. Before the issuance of this IFRS, the disclosure requirements were contained within IAS 32. IAS 32 now contains just the presentation requirements of financial instruments.

This IFRS applies to all entities, including entities that have few financial instruments (e.g. simply receivables and payables).

In order to enable users to evaluate the effect of financial instruments in an entity's financial statements, IFRS 7 requires the following disclosures to be contained within the financial statements:

- the significance of financial instruments for the entity's financial position and performance; and

- the nature and extent of risks arising from financial instruments to which the entity is exposed during the period and at the end of the reporting period and how the entity manages those risks.

IFRS 7 also requires qualitative and quantitative information about the entity's exposure to risk.

Qualitative Disclosures

The qualitative disclosures describe management's objectivies, policies and processes for managing those identified risks.

Quantitative Disclosures

The quantitative disclosures provide the information needed about the extent to which the entity is exposed to risk based on information provided internally to the entity's key management personnel.

In addition, IFRS 7 requires specific minimum disclosures about credit risk, liquidity risk and market risk.

IFRS 8
Operating Segments

OBJECTIVE

The objective of this IFRS is to deal with the information that an entity should disclose in its financial statements to enable users to evaluate the nature and financial effects of the business activities and the economic environment in which the business operates.

The standard itself deals with two segments:

- 'reportable' segments; and

- 'operating' segments.

A reportable segment is an operating segment or aggregations of operating segments that meet specified criteria.

Operating segments are components of an entity about which separate financial information is available that is evaluated regularly by the chief operating decision maker in deciding how to allocate resources and in assessing performance. The chief operating decision maker could be the chief executive or some other senior official.

IFRS 8 requires a reporting entity to disclose in their financial statements a measure of operating segment profit or loss and of segment assets. The IFRS also requires a reconciliation of total reportable segment revenues, total profit or loss, total assets, liabilities and other amounts disclosed within the financial statements for reportable segments to corresponding amounts in the entity's financial statements.

The IFRS also requires an entity to report information about the revenues it derives from its products or services and disclose information concerning the countries in which it earns revenues. In addition, the IFRS requires descriptive information to be disclosed concerning the way the operating segments were determined as well as the products and services provided by the segments, the differences between the measurements used in reporting segment information and those used in the entity's financial statements as well as changes in the measurement of segment amounts from period to period.

IAS 1
Presentation of Financial Statements

OBJECTIVE

The objective of IAS 1 is to deal with the basis on which an entity presents its general purpose financial statements and the composition of those financial statements.

A complete set of general purpose financial statements of an entity (prepared at least annually) should comprise the following:

- a statement of financial position as at the end of the period;

- a statement of comprehensive income for the period;

- a statement of changes in equity for the period;

- a statement of cash flows for the period; and

- notes to the financial statements.

Illustration

Ethan Inc
Statement of Financial Position as at 31 December 2008

	$
ASSETS	
Non-current assets	
Property, plant and equipment	X
Goodwill	X
Investments	X
Available-for-sale investments	<u>X</u>
	X
Current assets	
Inventories	X
Trade and other receivables	X
Other current assets	X
Cash and cash equivalents	<u>X</u>
	X
Total Assets	X

EQUITY AND LIABIILTIES

Share capital	X
Other reserves	X
Retained earnings	X
	X
Non-controlling interests	X

Non-current liabilities

Long-term loans	X
Deferred tax	X
Obligations under finance leases	X
	X

Current liabilities

Trade and other payables	X
Short-term loans	X
Current tax	X
	X
Total Equity and Liabilities	X

Ethan Inc
Statement of Comprehensive Income for the period ended 31 December 2008

	2008	2007
Revenue	X	X
Cost of sales	(X)	(X)
Gross profit	X	X
Distribution costs	(X)	(X)
Administrative expenses	(X)	(X)
Other expenses	(X)	(X)
Finance costs	(X)	(X)
Profit before tax	X	X
Income tax expense	(X)	(X)
Profit for the year from continuing operations	X	X

Other comprehensive income:

Exchange differences on translation of foreign Operations	X	X
Gains on property revaluation	X	X
Actuarial gains (losses) on defined benefit pension scheme	X	X
Other comprehensive income for the year net of tax	X	X
Total comprehensive income for the year net of tax	<u>X</u>	<u>X</u>

Ethan Inc
Statement of Changes in Equity for the year ended 31 December 2008

	Share Capital	Retained Earnings	Revaluation Reserve	Total
Opening balance at 1 January 2008	X	X	X	X
Total comprehensive income for the year		X		X
Revaluation gain			X	X
Issue of share capital	X			X
Dividends		(X)		(X)
Balance as at 31 December 2008	X	X	X	X

We shall discuss the statement of cash flows in IAS 7 'Cash Flow Statements' (see page 30).

When an entity prepares financial statements that comply with the IFRSs then an entity is required to make an explicit and unreserved disclosure of such within their financial statements. An entity cannot make such an explicit and unreserved disclosure of compliance with IFRS if they do not comply with all the requirements of IFRS.

The Concept of Going Concern

The concept of going concern is central to the basis of determining whether the financial statements should be prepared on a going concern basis or not. When preparing financial statements, management must make an assessment of the entity's ability to continue as a going concern. If management do not intend to liquidate or cease trading then management should prepare the financial statements on a going concern basis.

However, where the management deems it necessary to liquidate or cease trading or has no other alternative but to do so, then the financial statements must not be prepared on a going concern basis.

Management must also disclose within the financial statements when they become aware of material uncertainties related to events or conditions that may cast significant doubt on the entity's ability to continue as a going concern.

Offsetting

An entity must present, separately, each material class of similar items and must not offset assets and liabilities, income or expense, unless required or permitted by an IFRS (e.g. IAS 20).

Accounting Policies

An entity must disclose information about significant accounting policies. It should also disclose the judgements (except those involving estimations) that management has made in the process of applying the entity's accounting policies and that have the most significant effect on the amounts recognised in the financial statements. Accounting policies should relate to the substance (commercial reality) of the amounts recognised in the financial statements.

IAS 2
Inventory

OBJECTIVE

IAS 2 prescribes the accounting treatment for inventories held by the entity at the end of a reporting period.

In summary, IAS 2 says the following:

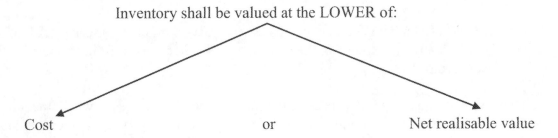

Inventory shall be valued at the LOWER of:

Cost   or   Net realisable value

Cost

IAS 2 states that 'cost' should comprise:

- the cost of purchase (e.g. the cost of raw materials);
- the costs of conversion (converting raw materials to finished goods); and
- other costs.

'Other costs' should only be recognised as those costs that have been incurred in bringing the inventories to their present location and condition.

Valuation

IAS 2 prescribes two possible valuation methods for inventories. An entity can adopt either:

- the first-in first-out basis (FIFO); or
- a weighted average basis.

Entities are not permitted to use a last-in first-out (LIFO) basis of valuation (this is where IAS 2 differs from UK GAAP SSAP 9 *'Stocks and Long-Term Contracts'* which allows LIFO to be used as a valuation basis.

Net Realisable Value

Net realisable value is the estimated selling price in the ordinary course of business, less the estimated costs of completion and the estimated costs necessary to make the sale.

Illustration

Kai Inc imports chemical products from overseas and the reporting date is 31 December 2008. At that date Kai undertakes an inventory count where inventory has been valued at the lower of cost or net realisable value in accordance with IAS 2. It has extracted details of the following chemical products as follows:

Product Number	Cost $	NRV $	Valuation $
556-009CCV	200.00	450.00	270.00
556-010CCV	150.00	340.00	150.00
556-011CCV	200.00	120.00	200.00

The first product valuation includes an element of administrative salaries because this product is highly valuable and involves a lot of extra administration work.

The second product appears to be fairly stated.

The third product is obsolete and management deem the net realisable to be nil.

Required

Based on the information above, determine the revised product values (where applicable) that should be included within the inventory valuation of Kai Inc as at 31 December 2008.

Solution

Product Number	Cost $	NRV $	Valuation $
556-009CCV	200.00	450.00	200.00 (W1)
556-010CCV	150.00	340.00	150.00
556-011CCV	200.00	nil	nil (W2)

W1
The administrative salary needs to be deducted because IAS 2 specifically states that general administrative overheads should be excluded from the costs of inventory valuation.

W2

Management's assessment is that the saleable value of this product is nil and this product needs to be written down to nil in order to accord with IAS 2 lower of cost or net realisable value principles.

IAS 7
Cash Flow Statements

OBJECTIVE

IAS 7 prescribes the provision of information that an entity should disclose about historical changes in cash and cash equivalents of an entity by means of a primary statement of cash flows. 'Cash' is cash on hand and 'on demand' deposits. 'Cash equivalents' are short-term, highly-liquid investments that are readily convertible to known amounts of cash and which are subject to insignificant risks of changes in value.

The statement of cash flows is a primary statement and as such needs to be given equal prominence as that of the statement of financial position (the balance sheet), the statement of comprehensive income (the income statement) and the statement of changes in equity.

Direct and Indirect Method

An entity can apply either the direct or indirect method of preparing its cash flow statements. IFRS does prefer the direct method, though the indirect method is a valid method.

The direct method involves major classes of gross receipts and gross cash payments being disclosed (i.e. taken 'direct' from the cash book), whilst the indirect method involves profit or loss being adjusted for the effects of transactions of a non-cash nature, any deferrals or accruals of past or future operating receipts or payments and items of income or expense associated with investing or financing cash flows.

Basis of Preparation

An entity needs to prepare a statement of cash flows using three headings:

- Operating Activities

- Investing Activities

- Financing Activities

Operating Activities
Operating activities are the principal day-to-date revenue-producing activities of the entity that are not investing activities or financing activities.

Investing Activities

Are the acquisition and disposal of long-term assets and other investments not included in cash equivalents.

Financing Activities

Are activities that result in the change and size of the contributed equity and borrowings of the entity.

Illustration

You are an accounts semi-senior at Collier & Co. a firm of Chartered Certified Accountants and are responsible for bringing a small portfolio of relatively high net-worth companies to draft stage for the manager to review.

You have been given the statement of comprehensive income and draft statements of financial position for a client, Zedcolour Trading Inc., for the year ended 31 December 2008, which are given below:

Zedcolour Trading Inc
Statement of Comprehensive Income for the year ended 31 December 2008

	$,000
Continuing Operations	
Revenue	31,461
Cost of sales	(16,304)
Gross profit	15,157
Loss on disposal of property, plant and equipment	(183)
Distribution costs	(5,663)
Administrative expenses	(3,681)
Profit from operations	5,630
Finance costs	(800)
Profit before tax	4,830
Income tax expense	(919)
Profit after tax	**3,911**

Zedcolour Trading Inc
Statement of Financial Position as at 31 December 2008

	2008 $000	2007 $000
Non-current assets		
Property, plant and equipment	29,882	19,100
Current assets		
Inventories	4,837	4,502
Trade and other receivables	5,244	4,978
Cash and cash equivalents	64	587
	10,145	10,067
Total assets	**40,027**	**29,167**
Current liabilities		
Trade and other payables	3,038	2,954
Tax	919	854
	3,957	3,808
Net current assets	**6,188**	**6,259**
Non-current liabilities		
Bank loans	10,000	7,000
Total liabilities	**13,957**	**10,808**
NET ASSETS	**26,070**	**18,359**
EQUITY		
Share capital	8,000	5,000
Share premium	2,500	1,000
Retained earnings (see note 1)	15,570	12,359
Total equity	**26,070**	**18,359**

Note 1

Retained earnings at 1 January 2008	12,359
Dividends	(700)
Profit for the year	3,911
Retained earnings at 31 December 2008	15,570

SOLUTION

ZEDCOLOUR TRADING INC
STATEMENT OF CASH FLOWS FOR THE YEAR ENDED 31 DECEMBER 2008

		$000	$000
Profit from operations		5,630	
Adjustments for:			
Depreciation		2,172	
Loss on disposal of property, plant and equipment		183	
Operating cash flows before movements in working capital		**7,985**	
Increase in inventories		(335)	
Increase in trade receivables		(266)	
Increase in trade payables		84	
Cash generated by operations		**7,468**	
Income taxes paid	(W1)	(854)	
Interest paid	(per SoCI)	(800)	
Net cash from operating activities			**5,814**
Investing Activities			
Proceeds from disposal of property, plant and equipment	(W2)	509	
Purchases of property, plant and equipment	(W3)	(13,646)	
Net cash used in investing activities			**(13,137)**
Financing Activities			
New bank loans raised		3,000	
Proceeds of share issue	(W4)	4,500	
Dividends paid		(700)	
Net cash used in/from financing activities			**6,800**

Net increase/(decrease) in cash and cash equivalents	**(523)**
Cash and cash equivalents at beginning of year	**587**
Cash and cash equivalents at the end of the year	**64**

Workings

W1 – Tax paid

Tax liability b/fwd	(854)
Tax charge per SoCI	(919)
Tax liability c/fwd	919
Balancing figure = tax paid	**854**

W2 – Proceeds from sale

NBV of assets sold	=	$692
Loss on sale	=	($183)
Proceeds	=	$509

W3 – Purchases of property plant and equipment

Opening balance = $19,200 less depreciation ($2,172) less net book value of assets sold (W2) ($692) plus additions (?) = closing balance of $29,882. Therefore ? = $13,646.

W4 – Proceeds from share issue

Balances b/f	-	share capital	(5,000)
	-	share premium	(1,000)
Balances c/f	-	share capital	8,000
	-	share premium	2,500
Balancing figure = proceeds received			4,500

IAS 8
Accounting Policies, Changes in Accounting Estimates and Errors

OBJECTIVE

The objective of this standard is to deal with how an entity should select its accounting policies, how it deals with changes within these accounting policies (and estimation techniques) and what to do when an error is discovered within the financial statements.

Accounting Policies

Accounting policies are the specific principles, bases, conventions, rules and practices applied by an entity in preparing and presenting its financial statements. In selecting their accounting policies, an entity must ensure that the policies used result in the financial statements providing reliable and relevant information about the effects of transactions or other events or conditions concerning the entity's financial position, performance and cash flows. In other words they should reflect the 'substance' of transactions.

Changes in Accounting Policy

IFRS allows management to change an accounting policy where the change will result in presenting more relevant and reliable information within the financial statements. Where an entity changes an accounting policy then the change must be applied retrospectively i.e. as if the revised policy had always been adopted. This means doing a prior-period adjustment so the comparative year is consistent. It would be pretty pointless in having amounts stated in the current year using one accounting policy but stated in the comparative year using a different accounting policy.

Changes in Estimation Techniques

A change in estimation technique is not a change in accounting policy. Changes in estimation techniques result from new information or new developments. The effects of a change in estimation technique is recognised prospectively (i.e. going forward) by way of inclusion in profit or loss in:

- the period of the change where the change affects that period only; or
- the period of change and future period, if the change affects both.

Error

Prior period errors are omissions from, and misstatements in, the entity's financial statements for one or more prior periods which have occurred as a result of failure to use, or misuse of reliable information that was available when the financial statements were prepared and could reasonably have been expected to have been obtained and taken into account in the preparation and presentation of those financial statements.

To correct an error in the prior period will result in a prior-period adjustment by restating the comparative amounts for the prior period(s) presented in which the error occurred or if the error occurred before the earliest period presented, by restating the opening balances of assets, liabilities and equity for the earlier prior period presented.

Illustration

Daniel Enterprises prepares its financial statements to 31 December each year. The following information has been decided upon before the preparation of the financial statements begins:

Daniel Enterprises will value its inventory on a weighted average basis this year as opposed to the traditional FIFO basis as the weighted average will result in more relevant and reliable information being presented.

The depreciation rates for property, plant and equipment will be changed from 20% straight line to 15% reducing balance as this represents a more relevant method of the entity's consumption of the assets.

Depreciation amounts are to be recognised in cost of sales as opposed to administrative expenses.

Required

Determine whether the above revisions are a change in accounting policy or a change in accounting estimate.

Solution

The revised inventory valuation is a change in accounting policy because the basis of valuation will be different in the current year. Daniel Enterprises should therefore restate the comparative year's inventory valuation and adjust its opening retained earnings in order that the financial statements are comparable and consistent.

The change in depreciation rates is a change of estimation technique. The entity is still consuming the asset, though at a slower rate than originally estimated. The initial recognition of the asset has not changed in amount and therefore this change should be recognised prospectively with no prior-period adjustment.

The change of classification of depreciation from expenses to cost of sales is a change in presentation, therefore a change in accounting policy. This adjustment is required to be made retrospectively.

IAS 10
Events after the Reporting Period

OBJECTIVE

The objective of this standard is to prescribe the accounting treatment and disclosure requirements for those events that are 'adjusting' events or 'non-adjusting' events.

Events after the reporting period are those events that are both favourable and unfavourable that occur between the end of the reporting period and the date on which the financial statements are authorised for issue.

Adjusting Event

An adjusting event is an event which occurs between the reporting date and the date on which the financial statements are authorised for issue and which provide evidence of conditions that existed at the reporting date which need to be taken into account in the financial statements.

Non-Adjusting Event

A non-adjusting event are conditions that arose after the reporting period but did not exist at the reporting date.

An adjusting event should be taken into account within the financial statements of the reporting entity. A non-adjusting event is disclosed within the notes to the financial statements.

Illustration

Norah Inc has prepared their financial statements for the year ended 31 December 2008. On 20 February 2009 a customer of theirs went into liquidation owing a material sum of money to Norah Inc.

On 28 February 2009, the main warehouse was burnt down in what is believed to be arson. The cost of rebuilding the warehouse is likely to be substantial.

Required

Identify whether the two events above are 'adjusting' or 'non-adjusting' events.

Solution

The bankruptcy of a customer so soon after the reporting date is a condition which existed at the reporting date so the financial statements will need to be adjusted to take account of the liquidation.

The warehouse fire is not an adjusting event as at the reporting date the event had not occurred. However, as the sums required to rebuild the warehouse are material, then Norah Inc should ensure that the following is disclosed within their financial statements:

- the nature of the event; and

- an estimate of its financial effect, or a statement that such an estimate cannot be made.

IAS 11
Construction Contracts

OBJECTIVE

The objective of this standard is to deal with the accounting treatment of revenue and costs associated with construction contracts. A standard was needed in this area because of the nature of construction contracts.

It is widely understood that some construction contracts can last for years and thus fall into different accounting periods. The problem is knowing how to recognise revenue and costs that fall into different accounting periods.

A construction contract is defined as a contract specifically negotiated for the construction of an asset or a combination of assets that are closely interrelated or interdependent in terms of their design, technology and function or their ultimate purpose or use.

Revenue

Contract revenue is measured at the fair value of the consideration received or receivable.

Contract Cost

Contract costs shall comprise:

- costs that relate directly to specific contracts;
- costs that are attributable to contract activity in general and can be allocated to the contract; and
- such other costs as are specifically chargeable to the customer under the terms of the contract.

Profit-Making Contracts

Where a contract is estimated to be profitable then revenue is recognised by reference to the stage of completion. Costs incurred in reaching the stage of completion are taken to the statement of comprehensive income (the income statement) as cost of sales. This is achieved by applying the percentage of completion to the total costs that are expected to occur over the life of the contract.

Loss-Making Contracts

Revenue is recognised by reference to the stage of completion. Cost of sales is the balancing figure to interact with the revenue that has been recognised to generate the required loss. For example, with a contract that is expected to make a loss of $100 and the contract revenue to be recognised is $80, then cost of sales is $180 to generate a loss of $100.

Uncertain Contracts

Where the outcome of a contract is uncertain, then no profit and no loss is recognised. Revenue to be recognised is the same as cost.

Percentage of completion method

The percentage of completion method is a method of accounting that recognises income on a contract as work progresses by matching contract revenue with contract costs incurred, based on the proportion of work completed.

The problem in dealing with the percentage of completion method lies in accurately deciphering the extent to which the projects are being finished and to assess the ability of the entity to actually bill and collect for the work done.

The percentage of completion method uses the contract account to accumulate costs and to recognise income. Under the provisions of IAS 11, income is not based on advances (cash collections) or progress billings. Any advances and progress billings are based on contract terms that do not necessarily measure contract performance.

Where costs and estimated earnings in excess of billings occurs, then the excess is classified as an asset. If billings exceed costs and estimated earnings, the difference is treated as a liability.

Double Entry

The double entry for contract revenue and costs is straight forward.

When costs are incurred on the contract:

DR   Contract account
CR   Cash/accruals/expenses

When amounts are billed:

DR   Receivables
CR   Contract account

To recognise revenue:

DR   Contract account
CR   Statement of comprehensive income (income statement)

To recognise costs:

DR   Statement of comprehensive income (income statement) – cost of sales
CR   Contract account

Rectification Costs

When mistakes occur during the course of the contract, these are referred to as 'rectification costs'. Such costs must be written off to profit or loss immediately as they occur.

Method to Deal with IAS 11

1. Calculate expected profits: contract price less costs to date less future costs
2. Calculate the stage of completion: either as a sales basis (value of work done to date / total sales value) or as a cost basis (costs to date / total costs).
3. Calculate revenue and costs for the year.

IAS 12
Income Taxes

OBJECTIVE

The objective of this standard is to deal with how an entity accounts for income tax (particularly current and deferred taxes). However, it also deals with all other taxes such as domestic and foreign taxes which are based on taxable profits. Income taxes also include withholding taxes.

Current Tax

Current tax expense should be estimated by an entity and recognised as a liability to the extent the current tax remains unpaid. Where the amount of current tax paid is in excess of the current tax expense, then the excess should be recognised as an asset. All current tax liabilities and assets must be measured at the amount expected to be paid (or recovered) from the taxation authorities using tax rates and laws that have been enacted or substantively enacted by the end of the reporting period.

Accounting for current tax is fairly straight forward. The problems arise when we come to look at deferred tax.

Deferred Tax

Deferred tax is essentially the differences inherent between accounting profit and taxable profit. Deferred tax is the future tax consequences based on the current period transactions.

Deferred Tax Assets

Deferred tax assets should be measured at the tax rates that are expected to apply to the period when the asset is realised. Deferred tax assets should only be recognised when it is deemed probable that there will be sufficient taxable profit in future periods to allow the benefit or part or all of that deferred tax asset to be used.

Deferred Tax Liabilities

Deferred tax liabilities should be measured at the tax rates that are expected to apply to the period when the liability is settled, based on tax rates and laws that have been enacted or substantively enacted at the end of the reporting period.

Discounting Deferred Tax Assets and Liabilities

The provisions in IAS 12 prohibit the discounting of deferred tax assets and liabilities.

Illustration

Leah Inc has an item of plant with a NBV of $6,000. The tax base (tax written down value) of the same asset is $5,000.

Required

Calculate the deferred tax asset or deferred tax liability that should be required in Leach Inc's financial statements. Leah Inc pays tax at a rate of 30%.

Solution

	Carrying Amount	Tax Base	Temporary Difference
	$6,000	$5,000	$1,000
Tax rate			x 30%
Deferred tax liability to be recognised			**$300**

Journal required:

DR   Income tax expense (statement of comprehensive income (income statement))
    CR   Deferred tax (statement of financial position (balance sheet))

IAS 16
Property, Plant and Equipment

OBJECTIVE

The objective of this standard is to prescribe the accounting treatment of an entity for their property, plant and equipment. It defines 'cost' and deals with how an entity should write off the cost of their property, plant and equipment. It also deals with when an entity should recognise 'subsequent expenditure' on existing property, plant and equipment in the statement of financial position (i.e. to 'capitalise' the subsequent expenditure) and when to write the subsequent expenditure off the to the statement of comprehensive income.

Initial Measurement

An entity is required to measure its property, plant and equipment at cost. Cost comprises:

- purchase price;
- import duties;
- non-refundable purchase taxes;
- costs directly attributable in bringing the asset to the location and condition necessary for it to be capable of operating in the manner intended; and
- initial estimate of the costs of dismantling and removing the item and restoring the site on which it is located (e.g. in onerous contracts).

Cost should also be net of trade discounts and rebates.

Subsequent Measurement

After initial recognition an entity can choose between the cost model or revaluation model for its accounting policy.

Cost Model
This is the most common. After initial recognition, the asset is simply carried at its original cost less accumulated depreciation and less any amounts recognised in respect of impairment.

Revaluation Model
After initial recognition, the asset is carried at its fair value with any increases or decreases in the fair value being recognised in other comprehensive income and accumulated in equity under the heading of 'revaluation surplus'. Any increases in fair

value shall only be recognised in profit or loss to the extent that it reverses a revaluation decrease of the same asset previously recognised in profit or loss.

Where an entity adopts the revaluation model then it must apply this model to all the assets in the same class.

Depreciation

Depreciation is the systematic allocation of the depreciable amount of an asset over its useful life. Depreciable amount is calculated as the cost of the asset, less its residual value. The residual value of an asset is the estimated amount that an entity would currently obtain from disposal of the asset after deducting the estimated costs of disposal.

Impairment

Impairments are dealt with under the provisions of IAS 36.

Illustration

Siobahn Inc purchases a new building for $200,000. Legal costs are incurred amounting to $2,000. The building is estimated to have a useful economic life of 50 years where the residual value is estimated to be $100,000.

Required

Calculate the amount to be recognised as property, plant and equipment together with the annual depreciation charges.

Solution

On initial recognition

IAS 16 says that 'cost' is purchase price plus any costs directly attributable in bringing the asset to the location and condition necessary for it to be capable of operating in the manner intended by management. Therefore, initial recognition:

DR   Property, plant and equipment ($200,000 + $2,000) $202,000
      CR   Cash $202,000

Depreciable amount is calculated as cost less residual value, so:

$202,000 less $100,000 / 50 years = $2,040 depreciation charge per year.

IAS 17

Leases

OBJECTIVE

The objective of this standard is to prescribe the accounting treatment for reporting entities for their operating and finance leases. It prescribes the situations when to include leases in the statement of financial position and when to include them in the statement of comprehensive income.

Operating Leases

An operating lease is a lease that is not a finance lease. Payments of such under an operating lease are charged to the statement of comprehensive income (income statement) on a straight-line basis over the lease term unless another systematic basis is more appropriate.

Finance Leases

The IASB stipulate that an entity's financial statements should report the economic substance of transactions as opposed to their legal form. IAS 17 is probably THE standard which perfectly illustrates this requirement.

At the commencement of the lease term, lessees shall recognise finance leases as assets and liabilities in the statement of financial position (balance sheet) at amounts equal to the fair value of the leased property or, if lower, the present value of the minimum lease payments determined at the inception of the lease.

Minimum lease payments are split between that of capital and that of interest (finance costs).

All finance leases give rise to assets which are to be subject to depreciation as per IAS 16 or IAS 38.

IAS 17 stipulates guidance that substantially all of the risks and rewards of ownership are passed to the lessee if any *one* of the following criteria are met:

1. The lease transfers ownership to the lessee at the end of the lease term.
2. The lease contains a bargain purchase option at the end of the lease term.
3. The lease term is for the major part of the asset's useful economic life.
4. The present value, at the inception of the lease, of the minimum lease payments is at least equal to substantially all of the fair value of the leased asset, net of

grants and tax credits to the lessor at that time (title may or may not eventually pass to the lessee).

5. The leased assets are of such a specialised nature that only the lessee can use them without modifications being made.

There are a further three indicators which may suggest that a lease might be properly considered as a finance lease.

1. If the lessee can cancel the lease, the lessor's associated costs with the cancellation are to be borne by the lessee.
2. Gains or losses arising from the fluctuation of fair value of the residual amount will accrue to the lessee.
3. The lessee has the ability to continue the lease for a supplemental term at a rent that is substantially lower than market rent (i.e. a 'peppercorn' rent).

Lessor Accounting

Operating Leases

Lessors are required to present assets that are subject to operating leases in the statement of financial position (balance sheet) according to the nature of the asset. Depreciation policies shall also be consistent with the normal depreciation for similar assets and calculated in accordance with the provisions of IAS 16 and IAS 38 where applicable. Lease income shall be recognised in income on a straight-line basis over the terms of the lease.

Finance Leases

Lessors should account for finance leases in their statement of financial position as a receivable at an amount equal to the net investment in the lease. Finance income is reflected at a constant periodic rate of return on the lessor's net investment in the finance lease.

IAS 18
Revenue

OBJECTIVE

This standard deals with how a reporting entity reports revenue in its financial statements and at which point revenue should be recognised within the financial statements. The standard deals with the following revenue streams and prescribes the situations when revenue should be recognised in respect of each.

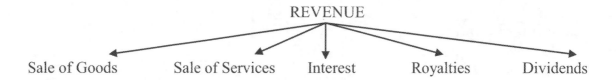

Sale of Goods

Revenue in respect of sales of goods should be recognised when the following criteria are met:

- the enterprise has transferred to the buyer the significant risks and rewards of ownership to the goods;
- the enterprise retains neither continuing managerial involvement to the degree normally associated with ownership nor effective control over the goods sold;
- the amount of revenue can be reliably measured;
- it is probable that the economic benefits associated with the transaction will flow to the enterprise; and
- the costs incurred or to be incurred in respect of the transaction can be measured reliably.

Sale of Services

Revenue in respect of sales of services should be recognised when the following criteria are met:

- the amount of revenue can be reliably measured;
- it is probable that the economic benefits associated with the transaction will flow to the entity;
- the stage of completion of the transaction at the reporting period can be measured reliably; and

- the costs incurred for the transaction and the costs to complete the transaction can be measured reliably.

Revenue from Interest

Revenue from interest should be recognised on a time-apportioned basis which reflects the effective yield on the asset.

Revenue from Royalties

Royalty revenue should be recognised on an accruals basis.

Revenue from Dividends

Revenue from dividends should be recognised when the right to receive payment has arisen.

IAS 19
Employee Benefits

OBJECTIVE

IAS 19 deals with how an entity should record transactions that fall under the scope of 'employee benefits'.

Employee benefits are all forms of consideration given by a reporting entity in exchange for the services rendered by its employees. The standard essentially deals with:

- short-term employee benefits
- post-employment benefits;
- other long-term employee benefits; and
- termination benefits.

Short-Term Employee Benefits

Short-term employee benefits are employee benefits which fall due within twelve months after the reporting period in which the employees render the related services.

In these respects, a reporting entity must recognise the undiscounted amount of short-term employee benefits for that service as a liability as at that date and as an expense unless another standard requires or permits the inclusion of the benefits in the cost of an asset (for example IAS 16). Where the amount already paid exceeds the undiscounted amount of the benefits, the excess is classed as an asset (e.g. a prepayment).

Post-Employment Benefits

These are sub-divided into two further classifications as follows:

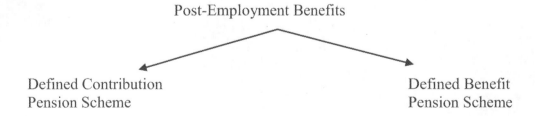

Post-Employment Benefits

Defined Contribution
Pension Scheme

Defined Benefit
Pension Scheme

Defined contribution schemes are post-employment benefit plans under which an entity pays fixed amounts of contributions into a separate fund. The employer has no further legal or constructive obligation to pay further contributions – even if the fund does not have sufficient assets to pay all the employee benefits.

The payments are simply charged to profit or loss as and when they arise.
Defined benefit pension schemes however are more complicated to account for. Defined benefit plans are post-employment plans other than defined contribution plans.

These sort of plans differ substantially from defined contribution plans because under the defined benefit plans an entity is obliged to provide the agreed benefits to current and former employees, even if the plan does not have sufficient assets.

In consequence, therefore, actuarial risk (i.e. that the benefits will cost more than expected) and investment risk fall, in substance, on the reporting entity. Notice how we have to report the 'substance'.

Accounting for defined benefit pension schemes is complicated. Actuarial information is needed to make a reliable estimate of the amount of benefit that employees have earned in return for their services. This benefit is then discounted using the Projected Unit Credit Method in order to determine the present value of the defined benefit obligation and the current service cost.

The charges to the statement of comprehensive income in respect of a defined benefit pension scheme will normally comprise:

Current service cost which is the increase in the present value of the schemes liabilities expected to arise from employee service in the current period.

Interest cost is the imputed cost caused by the unwinding of discount because scheme liabilities are closer to settlement.

Past service cost is the increase in the present value of the scheme liabilities relate to employee service in prior periods as a result of either new retirement benefits or improvements to the existing retirement benefits.

Expected return on plan assets is the increase in the market value of the plan assets.

Actuarial gains or losses are changes in actuaries assumptions and can be recognised in the statement of comprehensive income if they exceed the 10% corridor.

Costs of settlement or curtailment are settlement transactions that relieve the employer, or the plan, of the responsibility for a pension benefit obligation or eliminate the risks to the employer or the plan. A curtailment is an event which significantly reduces the expected years of future service of present employees or eradicates (for a substantial number of employees) the accrual of defined benefits for some or all of their future services, for example the termination of contracts for services.

Illustration

Westhead Trading Inc reports under IFRS and operates a Defined Benefit Pension Scheme for its employees. The scheme is reviewed on an annual basis and the actuaries have provided the following information:

	31 March 2007	31 March 2008
	$,000	$,000
Present value obligation	1,500	1,750
Fair value of plan assets	1,500	1,650
Current service cost to 31 March 2008		160
Contributions paid to 31 March 2008		85
Benefits paid to employees to 31 March 2008		125
Unrecognised gains at 1 April 2007	200	
Expected return on plan assets at 1 April 2007	12%	
Discount rate for plan liabilities at 1 April 2007	10%	

The average remaining working lives of Westhead Trading Inc employees as at 31 March 2007 is 10 years.

Required

Prepare extracts of the financial statements for Westhead Trading Inc as at 31 March 2008.

Solution

Financial Statement Extracts

Statement of Comprehensive Income

	£,000
Current service cost	160
Interest cost (10% x 1,500)	150
Expected return on plan assets (12% x 1,500)	(180)
Recognised actuarial gain in year (see below)	(5)
Costs per statement of comprehensive income	**125**

Statement of Financial Position

Present value of obligation	1,750
Fair value of plan's assets	(1,650)
	100
Unrecognised actuarial gains (see ^ below)	140
Liability per statement of financial position	**240**

^ Movement in unrecognised actuarial gain:

Unrecognised actuarial gain at 1 April 2007	200
Actuarial gain on plan assets (W1)	10
Actuarial loss on plan liability (W1)	(65)
Gain recognised (W2)	(5)
Unrecognised actuarial gain at 31 March 2008	140

WORKINGS

W 1

		Plan Assets $,000	Plan Liabilities $,000
Balance at 1 April 2007		1,500	1,500
Current service cost			160
Interest			150
Expected return		180	
Contributions paid		85	
Benefits paid to employees		(125)	(125)
Actuarial Gain	β	10	
Actuarial Loss	β		65
		1,650	1,750

W 2

Net unrecognised actuarial gains at 1 April 2007	200
10% corridor (10% x 1,500)	150
Excess	50 ÷ 10 years = $5,000 gains to be recognised

Other Long-Term Employee Benefits

Other long-term employee benefits are any other employee benefits which do not fall due within twelve months after the end of the reporting period in which the employees render the related service.

Under these types of employee benefits, an entity can recognise actuarial gains and losses and past service cost immediately.

Termination Benefits

Termination benefits are recognised as a liability and as an expense when, and only when, the entity is demonstrably committed to either:

- terminate the employment of an employee or group of employees before the normal retirement date; or
- provide termination benefits as a result of an offer made in order to encourage voluntary redundancy.

Any termination benefits which fall due more than 12 months after the end of the reporting period must be discounted to present day values.

IAS 20
Accounting for Government Grants and Disclosure of Government Assistance

OBJECTIVE

The objective of this standard is to prescribe the accounting treatment and the disclosure requirements of an entity who has received government grants and/or government assistance. Government grants could be given to entities for (say) setting up in business in a deprived area to provide employment.

Government Grants

Government grants are assistance by government in the form of transfers of resources (usually in the form of economic benefits) to an entity in return for past or future compliance with stipulated terms relating to the operating activities of the entity.

Government Assistance

Government assistance is action by the government designed to provide an economic benefit specific to an entity or range of entities qualifying under certain criteria.

Government Grants: Recognition

Government grants must not be recognised within the entity's financial statements until there is reasonable assurance that:

(a) the entity will comply with the terms and conditions attached to the grant(s); and
(b) the grant will be received by the entity.

There are generally two forms of government grant:

Capital based grants are grants from the government whose primary condition is that an entity qualifying to receive the grant should purchase, construct or otherwise acquire a long-term asset.

Capital based grants can be treated in two ways:

DR   Cash
      CR   Deferred income

In this example, the grant will be released to the statement of comprehensive income (income statement) over the life of the grant.

DR   Cash
     CR   Non-current asset

In this example, the grant is deducted in arriving at the carrying value of the asset to be recognised. The grant is recognised in the statement of comprehensive income (income statement) via reduced depreciation charges.

Repayable Grants

Where grants are repayable then repayment of a grant related to income shall be applied first against any unamortised deferred income in the statement of financial position (balance sheet). Where there is no unamortised deferred income then it shall be recognised immediately as an expense.

Where capital based grants are concerned, repayment of a grant related to an asset shall be recorded by increasing the carrying amount of the asset or reducing the amount of deferred income balance by the amount payable.

IAS 21
The Effects of Changes in Foreign Exchange Rates

OBJECTIVE

The objective of this standard is to prescribe how an entity, who carries on foreign activities will account for the effects of changes in foreign exchange rates.

The first thing an entity is required to do is to determine the functional currency of the entity. The functional currency is the currency of the primary economic environment in which it operates (e.g. sterling). In determining the functional currency, an entity is required to consider the following factors:

- the currency that mainly influences sales prices for goods and services (this will often be the currency in which sales prices for its goods and services are denominated and settled); and
- of the country whose competitive forces and regulations mainly determine the sales prices of its goods and services.

In addition, an entity will normally consider the currency that mainly influences labour, material and other costs of providing goods or services.

Foreign Currency Transactions

Foreign currency transactions should be recorded initially in the functional currency by using the exchange rate at the date of the transaction.

At the end of the reporting period, an entity should translate foreign currency monetary items of assets and liabilities using the closing rate at the reporting date. Non-monetary items shall be translated using the exchange rate at the date of the transaction.

Non-monetary items that are measured using fair values in a foreign currency should be translated using the exchange rates at the date when the fair value was determined.

Any exchange differences on translation are recognised in profit or loss in the period in which they arise.

Exchange differences that arise on a monetary item that forms part of a reporting entity's net investment in a foreign operation must be recognised in profit or loss in the separate financial statements of the reporting entity or the individual financial statements of the foreign operation, as appropriate. In the consolidated financial statements exchange differences shall be recognised initially in other comprehensive income and reclassified from equity to profit or loss on disposal of the net investment.

Presentation of Information Where the Functional Currency is Different from the Presentational Currency

Where an entity's presentational currency differs from its functional currency then it should translate its results and financial position into the presentational currency.

IAS 23
Borrowing Costs

OBJECTIVE

The objective of this standard is to prescribe the treatment that an entity should follow in dealing with borrowing costs associated with the acquisition, construction or production of a qualifying asset. The fundamental aspect to this standard is determining a *qualifying* asset.

Borrowing costs are interest and other costs that an entity incurs in connection with the borrowing of funds.

The standard requires that an entity should capitalise borrowing costs that are directly attributable to the acquisition, construction or production of a qualifying asset. A qualifying asset is an asset that takes a substantial period of time to get ready for its intended use or sale. The words 'substantial period' are fundamental to this standard. If the asset does not take a substantial period of time then the associated borrowing costs would not qualify for capitalisation.

Examples of qualifying assets include:

- manufacturing plant
- investment properties
- intangible assets

Capitalisation Rate

The capitalisation rate which borrowings are capitalised must be the weighted average of the borrowing costs applicable to the borrowings of the entity that are outstanding during the period, other than borrowings made specifically for the purpose of obtaining a qualifying asset. The amount of borrowing costs that an entity capitalises in a period must not exceed the amount of borrowing costs it incurred during that period.

The capitalisation of borrowing costs commences when the following conditions are met:

- the entity incurs expenditure for the asset;
- it incurs borrowing costs; and
- it undertakes activities that are necessary to prepare the asset for its intended use or sale.

When an entity suspends active development of a qualifying asset, it must suspend capitalisation of borrowing costs.

Illustration

Smyth Inc has three sources of borrowings in the period:

	Outstanding liability $,000	Interest charge $,000
7 year loan	8,000	1,000
25 year loan	12,000	1,000
Bank overdraft	4,000 (average)	600

Required:

Requirement A
Calculate the appropriate capitalisation rate if all of the borrowings are used to finance the production of a qualifying asset but none of the borrowings relate to a specific qualifying asset.

Requirement B
If the 7 year loan is an amount which can be specifically identified with a qualifying asset calculate the rate which should be used on the other assets.

Solution

A
$$\frac{1,000,000 + 1,000,000 + 600,000}{8,000,000 + 12,000,000 + 4,000,000}$$

$$= 10.833\%$$

B
$$\frac{1,000,000 + 600,000}{12,000,000 + 4,000,000}$$

$$= 10\%$$

IAS 24
Related Party Disclosures

OBJECTIVE

This standard ensures that transactions with related parties are adequately disclosed within an entity's financial statements. IAS 24 is a wholly disclosure standard.

Related Parties

A party is related to an entity if:

(a) directly, or indirectly through one or more intermediaries, the party:
   (i)   controls, is controlled by, or is under common control with, the entity (this includes parents, subsidiaries and fellow subsidiaries);
   (ii)   has an interest in the entity that gives it significant influence over the entity; or
   (iii) has joint control over the entity;
(b) the party is an associate (as defined in IAS 28 *Investments in Associates*) of the entity;
(c) the party is a joint venture in which the entity is a venturer (IAS 31 *Interests in Joint Ventures)*;
(d) the party is a member of the key management personnel of the entity or its parent;
(e) the party is a close member of the family of any individual referred to in (a) or (d);
(f) the party is an entity that is controlled, jointly controlled or significantly influenced by, or for which significant voting power in such entity resides with, directly or indirectly, any individual referred to in (d) or (e); or
(g) the party is a post-employment benefit plan for the benefit of employees of the entity, or of any entity that is a related party of the entity.

IAS 24 is purely a disclosure standard and it requires an entity to disclose the following information if there have been transactions between related parties:

(a) the amount of the transactions;
(b) the amount of outstanding balances and:
   (i) their terms and conditions, including whether they are secured, and the nature of the consideration to be provided in settlement; and
   (ii) details of any guarantees given or received;
(c) provisions for doubtful debts related to the amount of outstanding balances; and
(d) the expense recognised during the period in respect of bad or doubtful debts due from related parties.

IAS 26
Accounting and Reporting by Retirement Benefit Plans

OBJECTIVE

This standard deals with the accounting and reporting by an entity who is involved in Retirement Benefit Plans.

A retirement benefit plan is an arrangement whereby an entity provides benefits for employees on or after termination of employment in the form of annual income or as a lump sum.

In the financial statements of an entity providing such a plan, they must contain a statement of net assets available for benefits and a description of the funding policy.

The financial statements should also contain either:

(a) a statement that shows:
    (i) the net assets available for benefits;
    (ii) the actuarial present value of promised retirement benefits, distinguishing between vested benefits and non-vested benefits; and
    (iii) the resulting excess or deficit; or
(b) a statement of net assets available for benefits including either:
    (i) a note disclosing the actuarial present value of promised retirement benefits, distinguishing between vested benefits and non-vested benefits; or
    (ii) a reference to this information in an accompanying actuarial report.

The financial statements of an entity providing retirement benefits must also explain the relationship between the actuarial present value of promised retirement benefits and the net assets available for the assets.

Retirement benefits must be carried at fair value. Marketable securities are carried at market value.

The financial statements of retirement benefit plans (whether defined benefit or defined contribution) must also contain:

- a statement of changes in net assets available for benefits;
- a summary of significant accounting policies; and
- a description of the plan and the effect of any changes in the plan during the period

IAS 27
Consolidated and Separate Financial Statements

OBJECTIVE

The objective of this standard is to enhance the relevance, reliability and comparability of a parent company in preparing their individual financial statements and consolidated financial statements.

Consolidated Financial Statements

A parent must consolidate its investments in subsidiaries. A subsidiary is an entity in which the parent has obtained control either through its holding in the subsidiaries equity share capital or by virtue of the parent's ability to influence the financial reporting and operational policies of the subsidiary.

Consolidation Procedure

All intra-group transactions must be eliminated from the consolidated financial statements. The consolidated financial statements must show the results of the group as a single economic entity.

Consolidated financial statements are prepared by combining the financial statements of parent and subsidiary line by line by adding together like items of assets, liabilities, equity, income and expenses.

The investment by the parent in the subsidiary is eliminated and accounted for in accordance with IFRS 3.

Non-controlling interests in the subsidiaries profit or loss are identified.

Non-controlling interests in the net assets of consolidated subsidiaries are identified separately from the parent's ownership in them and are presented in the consolidated statement of financial position (balance sheet) within equity, separately from the equity of the owners of the parent. In addition, total comprehensive income must be attributed to the owners of the parent and the non-controlling interests.

Separate Financial Statements

Where an entity elects to, or is required by regulation, to present separate financial statements then any investment in subsidiaries must be accounted for in accordance with IAS 39 *Financial Instruments: Recognition and Measurement*.

IAS 28
Investments in Associates

OBJECTIVE

The objective of this standard is to prescribe the accounting treatment that an entity who has investments in associates should adopt.

Where an investing company holds 20% or more of the voting power of an investee, then this means that they hold 'significant influence'. Significant influence is the power to participate in the financial and operating policy decisions of the investee. If, however, they own more than 50% of the voting rights, then this gives rise to a subsidiary that requires consolidation in accordance with IAS 27.

Equity Method

Investments in associates are accounted for using the equity method of accounting. This method states that the investment in the associate is initially recognised at cost and the carrying amount of the investment is increased or decreased in order to recognise the investor's share of the profit or loss of the investee after the associate has been acquired.

Where the associate pays dividends to the investor, then these reduce the carrying amount of the investment.

Where the associate revalues their property or has foreign exchange translation differences, then these will also give rise to an adjustment to the carrying amount of the investment for the investor's proportionate interest - such changes being recognised in the investee's other comprehensive income.

The investor's financial statements must also follow uniform accounting policies for like transaction and events of its investee.

Illustration

IAS 28 states the value of an investment in an associate should be:

Cost + share of associate's post acquisition profit or loss

Cost is the share of associates net assets at the date of acquisition + goodwill

---

Thus:

carrying value = share of net assets at acquisition + goodwill + share of post acquisition profit or loss, which is the same as:

Share of net assets at balance sheet date + goodwill

IAS 29
Financial Reporting in Hyperinflationary Economies

OBJECTIVE

This standard deals with the accounting requirements for those entities whose functional currency is the currency of a hyperinflationary economy.

Hyperinflation is inflation that is out of control. The financial statements of an entity whose functional currency is the currency of a hyperinflationary economy must be stated in terms of the measuring unit current at the end of the reporting period. If the financial statements are not restated and are reported in a hyperinflationary economy then they will clearly be unreliable.

Financial statements need to be restated with the use of a general price index that reflects changes in general purchasing power.

Illustration

Restatement of the financial statements should be as follows:

Non-monetary items carried at cost or cost less depreciation (also known as 'depreciated historic cost') should be restated by applying the change in general price index from the date of acquisition to the reporting date to the historical cost and accumulated depreciation.

Non-monetary items carried at revaluation should be restated by applying the change in general price index to their revalued amount from the date of revaluation to the reporting date.

Monetary items do not need to be restated because, by definition, they are already expressed in the monetary unit current at the reporting date.

When an economy ceases to be hyperinflationary and an entity ceases to use the provisions in IAS 29, then it shall treat the amounts expressed in the measuring unit current at the end of the previous reporting period as the basis for the carrying amount in the subsequent financial statements.

IAS 31
Interests in Joint Ventures

OBJECTIVE

This standard deals with those entities that have interests in joint ventures and prescribes the accounting for such interests.

Joint Venture

A joint venture is a contractual arrangement where two or more parties are involved in an undertaking that is subject to joint control. Joint control is contractually agreed and involves the sharing of control over an activity. A joint venture can only be classified as such if the financial and operating decisions relating to the activity requires the unanimous consent of the parties sharing the control.

There are three types of joint venture that are dealt with in IAS 31:

- jointly-controlled operations;
- jointly-controlled assets; and
- jointly-controlled entities.

Jointly-Controlled Operations

In these joint ventures, each venture uses its own property, plant and equipment and carries its own inventories. It incurs its own expenses and liabilities and raises its own finance. The financial statements of a venture will include:

- the assets that it controls and the liabilities that it incurs; and
- the expenses that it incurs and its share of the income that it earns from the sale of goods or services by the joint venture.

Jointly-Controlled Assets

In respect of jointly-controlled assets, a venture must recognise in their financial statements:

- its share of the jointly-controlled assets, classified according to the nature of the assets;
- any liabilities that it has incurred;
- its share of any liabilities incurred jointly with the other venturers in relation to the joint venture;

- any income from the sale or use of its share of the output of the joint venture, together with its share of any expenses incurred by the joint venture; and
- any expenses that it has incurred in respect of its interest in the joint venture.

Jointly-Controlled Entities

This type of entity involves the establishment of a separate entity in which each venture has an interest. IAS 31 allows two possible methods of recognition of jointly-controlled entities in a venturer's financial statements:

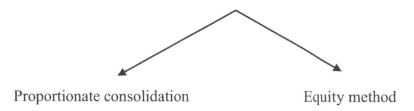

Proportionate consolidation   Equity method

Proportionate Consolidation

This involves a venturer's share of each of the assets, liabilities, income and expenses of a jointly-controlled entity is combined on a line by line basis with like items in the venturer's financial statements, or reported as separate line items in the venturer's financial statements.

Equity Method

This method involves the venturer initially recording the jointly-controlled entity at cost and then adjusted for the post-acquisition change in the venturer's share of net assets of the jointly-controlled entity.

IAS 32
Financial Instruments: Presentation

OBJECTIVE

The objective of this standard is to prescribe the presentation of financial instruments as either debt or equity transactions. Disclosure requirements in respect of financial instruments are found in IFRS 7.

Financial Instrument

A financial instrument is any contract that gives rise to a financial asset of one entity and a financial liability in another entity. They can be either financial assets, financial liabilities or equity instruments.

Financial Assets

A financial asset is any asset that is:

(a) cash;
(b) an equity instrument of another entity;
(c) a contractual right:
    (i) to receive cash or another financial asset from another entity; or
    (ii) to exchange financial assets or financial liabilities with another entity under conditions that are potentially favourable to the entity; or
(d) a contract that will or may be settled in the entity's own equity instruments and is:
    (i) a non-derivative for which the entity is or may be obliged to receive a variable number of the entity's own equity instruments; or
    (ii) a derivative that will or may be settled other than by the exchange of a fixed amount of cash or another financial asset for a fixed number of the entity's own equity instruments. For this purpose the entity's own equity instruments do not include instruments that are themselves contracts for the future receipt or delivery of the entity's own equity instruments.

Financial Liabilities

A financial liability is any liability that is:

(a) a contractual obligation:
    (i) to deliver cash or another financial asset to another entity; or
    (ii) to exchange financial assets or financial liabilities with another entity under conditions which are potentially unfavourable to the entity; or

(b) a contract that will or may be settled in the entity's own equity instruments and is:
    (i) a non-derivative for which the entity is or may be obliged to deliver a variable number of the entity's own equity instruments; or
    (ii) a derivative that will or may be settled other than by the exchange of a fixed amount of cash or another financial asset for a fixed number of the entity's own equity instruments. For this purpose the entity's own equity instruments do not include instruments that are themselves contracts for the future receipt or delivery of the entity's own equity instruments.

Equity Instruments

An equity instrument is any contract that evidences a residual interest in the assets of an entity after deducting all of its liabilities.

Where a financial instrument has a redemption feature or requires an entity to deliver cash or another financial asset, then this is a financial liability and should be recognised as such within the financial statements.

Where financial instruments do not have redemption features or the entity does not have an obligation to deliver cash (either to redeem the instrument or in the form of interest or dividends) then they are recognised as equity.

Where an entity reacquires its own equity instruments, those instruments are deducted from equity. No gain or loss is recognised in profit or loss on the purchase, sale or cancellation of an entity's own equity instruments. Any consideration paid or received must be recognised directly in equity.

Any interest payments, dividends, losses and gains relating to financial instruments or a component of a financial instrument that has been recognised as financial liability must be recognised as income or expense in profit or loss.

Distributions (dividends) to holders of an equity instrument must be debited directly to equity net of any related income tax benefit.

Illustration

Michelle Inc issues preference shares to shareholders that pay 10% dividends on an annual basis.

The preference shares contain an obligation to pay cash to the preference shareholders and they should be classified as a financial liability. The 10% dividends should be recognised as a finance cost (interest) in Michelle Inc's statement of comprehensive income.

IAS 33
Earnings per Share

OBJECTIVE

The objective of IAS 33 is to prescribe the calculation and disclosure of an entity's earnings per share.

The scope of this standard applies to the separate financial statements whose debt or equity instruments are publicly traded (or are in the process of being issued in a public market). It also applies to the consolidated financial statements of a group whose parent is required to apply this standard to its separate financial statements.

Basic Earnings per Share

The calculation of basic EpS is straight forward. It is arrived at by dividing the profit (or loss) relating to the ordinary shareholders by the weighted average number of ordinary shares outstanding in the period.

Illustration

Jones Inc has 1,000,000 shares in issue. The profit for the year ended 31 December 2008 (adjusted for the post-tax effect of preference dividends and minority interests) was $200,000.

Required

Calculate the basic EpS.

Solution

EpS Calculation = Profit ÷ ordinary shares

So $200,000 ÷ 1,000,000 = 20c

Preference Dividends

There are generally two types of preference dividend:

- a cumulative preference dividend; and
- a non-cumulative preference dividend

Cumulative Preference Dividend

If no dividend is declared in respect of a reporting period, the holders accumulate their rights.

Non-Cumulative Preference Dividend

If no dividend is declared then the holder(s) of the preference shares lose the right to the dividend.

Note – profit or loss will only be adjusted for preference dividends declared in the reporting period.

Weighted Average Number of Shares

The basic rule in IAS 33 is that the number of ordinary shares is the weighted average number of ordinary shares outstanding for the period. It follows, therefore, that the number of shares in existence at the beginning of the reporting period be adjusted for shares that have been issued for cash or other forms of consideration during the period.

Illustration

Bury Inc financial reporting period is 1 January 2008 to 31 December 2008. On 1 January 2008 it had 100 ordinary shares in issue. On 31 March 2008 it issued a further 50 shares.

Required:

Calculate the weighted average number of ordinary shares in issue.

Solution

Before the issue
100 ordinary shares x 3 / 12   25

After the issue
150 ordinary shares x 9 / 12   <u>113</u>

Weighted average   138

There are occasions when shares are issued but no consideration is received. Such circumstances can arise due to:

- bonus issues; and
- rights issues.

Bonus Issues

A bonus issue is always treated as if the shares issued in the bonus issue had been in issue for the whole of the reporting period.

Illustration

Bolton Inc issues a bonus share issue of 1 share for every 10.

The bonus fraction becomes:

$$\frac{10 + 1}{10} = \frac{11}{10}$$

Rights Issues

A rights issue gives the shareholder the right to buy further shares from the company at a price which is set below that of market value. A rights issue has two inherent advantages:

- the company will receive a consideration which will boost earnings; and
- the shareholder receives part of the consideration for no consideration due to the fact it is deliberately set below market value for the shares in the rights issue.

Because of this a bonus fraction is applied to the number of shares in issue before the date of the rights issue and the new shares issued are pro-rated as for issues for consideration.

The bonus fraction is the cumulative-rights (cum-rights) price per share ÷ the theoretical ex-rights price per share.

Note: the theoretical ex-rights price is abbreviated to 'TERP'.

Illustration

Bart Inc has 1,000 shares in issue on 1 January 2008. On 31 March 2008 it issues a rights issue for 1 share for every 5 held at 90c. The market value of the shares at 31 March 2008 were $1 (cum-rights).

Required

Calculate the number of shares for use in the EpS calculation.

Solution

	Number
1 January to 31 March	
1,000,000 x 3/12 x 1/0.9833	254,237
1 April to 31 December	
1,200,000 x 9/12	900,000
	1,154,237

Rights Issue Bonus Fraction

	Shares	$	$
	5	1	5.0
	1	0.9	0.9
	6		5.9

Theoretical Ex-Rights Price

$$5.9 \div 6 \qquad = 0.9833$$

Bonus Fraction
(cum-rights price per share
÷ TERP)

$$= \dfrac{1}{0.9833}$$

Note

Where bonus issues are issued in a reporting period, then an entity must restate the comparative year to account for the bonus issue in order to ensure the financial statements achieve consistency.

Multiple Changes in Capital in the Period

Sometimes an entity could issue a mixture of bonus and rights issue or even issue further shares at full market price.

To deal with these it is important that you apply the following method:

- Make a note of the number of shares in issue at the start of the year.
- Look forward during the year and note the total number of shares after each capital change.
- Multiply each number by the fraction of the year that it was in existence (e.g. 3/12ths).

- Where the entity issues a bonus issue, multiply all the previous slices by the bonus fraction.

Diluted Earnings per Share

Diluted earnings per share is calculated to inform existing shareholders that this could potentially occur. It acts to give notice to the shareholders that there may be potential ordinary shareholders who may also become shareholders in the future. This could occur, for example, where an entity has convertible debt (i.e. a loan that could be converted to shares in the future).

The new number of ordinary shares should be the weighted average number of shares used in the basic EpS calculation PLUS the weighted average number of ordinary shares which would be issued on the conversion of all the dilutive potential ordinary shares into ordinary shares.

Illustration

Using the numbers in the first illustration (Jones inc) assume that on 31 March 2008 Jones Inc issues $200,000 6% convertible debt. The terms of the conversion are:

1. 100 shares / $100 if within 5 years
2. 110 shares / $100 if after 5 years

Jones inc pays tax at 30%

	Number of Shares	Profit $
Basic	1,000,000	200,000
Dilution:		
Shares: $\frac{200,000}{100} \times 110 \times \frac{9}{12}$	165,000	
Interest:		
$\frac{\$200,000 \times 6\% \times 9 \times 0.70}{12}$		6,300
	1,165,000	206,300

EpS = ($206,300 ÷ 1,165,000 shares in issue)   =   **17.71c**

Where to Present EpS

Basic and diluted EpS should be presented on the face of the statement of comprehensive income for:

- the profit or loss from continuing operations; and
- the profit or loss for the period; and
- each class of ordinary shares that has a different right to share in the net profit for the period.

IAS 34
Interim Financial Reporting

OBJECTIVE

The objective of this standard is to deal with the minimum content of a set of interim financial reports as well as outline the principles for recognition and measurement in a complete or reduced set of financial statements for an interim period.

Interim Financial Reports

Interim financial reports are reports that contain either a complete set of financial statements or a set of condensed financial statements for an interim period. An interim period for the purposes of IAS 34 is a financial reporting period which is shorter than a full financial year.

Minimum Content Requirements

As a minimum, an interim financial report must include the following:

(a) a condensed statement of financial position;
(b) a condensed statement of comprehensive income, presented as either;
    (i) a condensed single statement; or
    (ii) a condensed separate income statement and a condensed statement of comprehensive income.
(c) a condensed statement of changes in equity;
(d) a condensed statement of cash flows; and
(e) selected explanatory notes.

Where an entity publishes a set of condensed financial statements then the condensed financial statements must include each of the headings and subtotals that were included in its most recent annual financial statements. Additional line items or notes must be included if their omission would render the interim financial statements misleading.

Materiality must be assessed in deciding how to recognise, measure and classify, or disclose an item for interim financial reporting purposes.

In terms of accounting policies, an entity who prepares interim financial statements must apply the same accounting policies that were applied in its annual financial statements except for policy changes made after the date of the most recent annual financial statements that are to be reflect in the next annual financial statements.

IAS 36
Impairment of Assets

OBJECTIVE

This standard prescribes the requirement to ensure that a reporting entity ensures its assets are carried at no more than their recoverable amount.

Impairment

An asset is impaired if its carrying amount in the financial statements exceeds the amount to be recovered through use or sale of the asset (its 'recoverable' amount).

RECOVERABLE AMOUNT IS THE *HIGHER* OF:

Fair value less costs to sell   Value in use

Fair value less costs to sell is the amount obtainable from the sale of an asset or cash-generating unit in an arm's length transaction between knowledgeable, willing parties, less the costs involved in the disposal.

Value in use is the present value of the future cash flows expected to be derived from an asset or cash-generating unit.

A *cash-generating unit* is the smallest identifiable group of assets that generates cash inflows that are largely independent of the cash inflows from other assets or groups of assets.

Intangible Assets

Intangible assets such as goodwill, intangible assets with indefinite useful lives and those intangible assets that are not yet available for use must be tested annually for impairment.

Recognising an Impairment Loss

An impairment loss must be recognised for a cash-generating unit in the following order:

- first to the goodwill in the group; then
- to the other assets of the unit on the basis of the carrying amount of each asset in the unit on a pro rata basis according to their carrying value.

Illustration

Shepland Laboratories Inc has the following net assets in its statement of financial position (balance sheet) as at 31 December 2008:

Statement of Financial Position (extract)

Non-current assets

Property	60
Plant	90
Goodwill	30
	180

In the board meeting the directors of Shepland Laboratories Inc, the directors have decided that the recoverable amount of the above assets amount to $135.

The impairment amounts to ($180 less $135) $45 and must be allocated first to goodwill, then to the rest of the assets in the CGU on a pro rata basis.

Solution

$30 of the impairment loss is allocated to the goodwill, reducing the carrying value of the goodwill to nil. $6 is allocated to the property with the remaining $9 being allocated to the plant.

Statement of Financial Position (extract)
Post Impairment

Non-current assets

Property	54
Plant	81
Goodwill	-
	135

Illustration

Poole Enterprises Inc has one of its many departments that performs machining operations on parts that are sold to contractors. A group of machines have an aggregate book value as at 31 December 2008 totalling $123,000. It has been determined by the directors of Poole Enterprises Inc that this group of machinery constitutes a CGU under IAS 36.

Upon analysis, the following facts about future expected cash inflows and outflows become apparent based on reduced productivity due to the age of the machinery and the increase in costs to generate output from the machines.

Year	Revenues	Costs (excluding depreciation)
	$	$
2009	75,000	28,000
2010	80,000	42,000
2011	65,000	55,000
2012	20,000	15,000
	240,000	140,000

After deducting the costs of disposal, the net selling price of each machine in the CGU is $84,500. This figure has been arrived at by using machinery quotations from a prominent dealer. Value in use is determined with reference to the above expected cash inflows and outflows which is discounted at a risk rate of 5%. This yields a present value of approximately $91,982 as shown below:

Year	Cash Flows	PV Factor	PV of Cash Flows
	$		$
2009	47,000	0.95238	44,761.91
2010	38,000	0.90703	34,467.12
2011	10,000	0.86384	8,638.38
2012	5,000	0.82270	4,113.51
			91,980.92*

*value in use

Since value in use exceeds net selling price ($84,500) value in use is selected to represent the recoverable amount of this CGU. This is lower than the carrying value of the group of assets and therefore an impairment loss should be recognised amounting to ($123,000 - $91,981) $31,019.

The impairment loss will be recognised as an operating expense as either depreciation or a separate heading in the statement of comprehensive income.

IAS 37
Provisions, Contingent Liabilities and Contingent Assets

OBJECTIVE

The objective of this standard is to ensure that appropriate recognition criteria are met before a reporting entity recognises a provision and to ensure sufficient disclosure is made to enable users to understand their nature, timing and amount.

Provision

A provision is a liability of an uncertain timing or amount.

Recognition of a Provision

A reporting entity can only recognise a provision within the financial statements if all three of the following criteria are met:

- the entity has a present obligation (legal or constructive) as a result of a past event;
- it is probable that an outflow of resources embodying economic benefits will be required to settle the obligation; and
- a reliable estimate can be made of the amount of the obligation.

Contingent Liabilities

A contingent liability is not recognised in the financial statements. Instead they are disclosed within the notes to the financial statements. A contingent liability is:

(a) a possible obligation that arises from past events and whose existence will be confirmed only by the occurrence or non-occurrence of one or more uncertain future events not wholly within the control of the entity; or
(b) a present obligation that arises from past events but is not recognised because:
   (i) it is not probable that an outflow of resources embodying economic benefits will be required to settle the obligation; or
   (ii) the amount of the obligation cannot be measured with sufficient reliability.

Contingent Assets

Only if the realisation of the asset is virtually certain will an entity recognise a contingent asset.

Illustration

Delta Inc has decided to close its maintenance department. It put a full announcement to the maintenance staff out on 20 November 2008. It has calculated the redundancy provisions and has included the redundancy provision in the financial statements for the year ended 31 December 2008.

Jolti Inc has made a provision for damages amounting to $10,000 in its financial statements for the year ended 31 December 2008 in respect of a legal case brought by one of its customers. The legal advisers have advised that they are not entirely certain as to the outcome of the case.

Solution

Delta
Delta has an obligation as a result of a past event (the announcement on 20 November 2008 of the redundancies).

It is probable (i.e. more likely than not) that an outflow of economic benefits will be required to settle the obligation (the redundancy payments).

It can reliably estimate the redundancy provision.

Therefore Delta can provide for the redundancy payments in the financial statements to 31 December 2008.

Jolti
Jolti should not recognise a provision for damages of $10,000 because it is not 'probable' that an outflow of resources will be required to settle. The legal advisers are not sure as to the outcome of the case.

Jolti should disclose the potential damages as a contingent liability in the financial statements to 31 December 2008.

IAS 38
Intangible Assets

OBJECTIVE

The objective of this standard is to deal with the accounting treatment for intangible assets that are not dealt with in other accounting standards.

Recognition of an Intangible Asset

An entity can only recognise an intangible asset when certain criteria are met.

An intangible asset must be recognised if, and only if:

- it is probable that the expected future economic benefits that are attributable to the asset will flow to the entity; and
- the cost of the asset can be measured reliably.

Intangible assets are recognised initially at cost. Cost comprises:

- the cost of purchase
- any import duties
- any irrecoverable taxes
- any directly attributable costs of preparing the asset for its intended use
- less any trade discounts and/or rebates.

Internally Generated Intangible Assets

An entity must not recognise any internally generated goodwill. Similarly, internally generated brands such as mastheads, publishing titles, customer lists and similar items in substance must also not be recognised as intangible assets. They should be treated as either research or development costs.

Expenditure on Research and Development

Research Expenditure
Any expenditure incurred during the research phase of a project must be recognised as an expense as and when it is incurred.

Development Expenditure

Once the research phase has been completed and the development phase commences, then any costs incurred during the development stage of a project must be capitalised if, and only if, an entity can demonstrate the following:

- the technical feasibility of completing the intangible asset so it will be available for use or sale;
- its intention to complete the intangible asset to either use it or sell it;
- the entity's ability to sell the intangible asset;
- how the entity can demonstrate that it will generate probable future economic benefits;
- the availability of resources in order to complete the intangible asset (resources include those of a technical and financial nature as well as other applicable resources to complete the intangible asset); and
- the entity's ability to measure the cost reliably.

Subsequent Measurement

After initial recognition, an entity can choose either the cost model or revaluation model for subsequent measurement.

Where an entity adopts the revaluation model then all the other intangible assets in its class must also be revalued unless there is no active market for those assets. An active market is where:

- the items traded in the market are homogenous;
- willing buyers and sellers can normally be found at any time; and
- prices are available to the public.

Intangible Assets with Indefinite Useful Lives

These are not amortised, they are reviewed for impairment in accordance with the provisions of IAS 36.

Intangible Assets with Finite Useful Lives

These are amortised on a systematic basis over their useful lives. The amortisation period and the amortisation method for an intangible asset with a finite useful life must be reviewed annually. If there is a change in the expected consumption of the intangible asset then the amortisation method must be changed accordingly and accounted for as a change in accounting estimate per IAS 8.

IAS 39
Financial Instruments: Recognition and Measurement

OBJECTIVE

The objective of this standard is to deal with the recognition and measurement of a financial asset, financial liability or other contracts to buy or sell non-financial items.

This standard is a companion standard to IAS 32 and IFRS 7.

Financial Assets

Financial assets contain four possible classifications within a set of financial statements, they can be:

- financial assets at fair value through profit or loss;
- held-to-maturity investments;
- loans and receivables; and
- available-for-sale financial assets.

Financial assets at fair value through profit or loss are classified as such if the financial asset is:

- held-for-trading; or
- was designated on initial recognition as one to be measured at fair value through profit or loss.

Held-to-maturity investments are non-derivative financial assets with fixed or determinable payments that an entity intends and is able to hold to maturity and which do not meet the definition of loans or receivables and upon initial recognition are not classified as assets at fair value through profit or loss or as available for sale.

Loans and receivables are non-derivative financial assets with fixed or determinable payments which are not quoted in an active market, not held for trading and not designated on initial recognition as assets at fair value through profit or loss or as available-for-sale.

Available-for-sale assets are non-derivative financial assets that do not meet any of the above criteria.

Financial Liabilities

Financial liabilities can be classified as:

- financial liabilities at fair value through profit or loss; or
- other financial liabilities measured at amortised cost using the effective interest method.

Initial Measurement

Financial assets and liabilities should be measured at fair value. Fair value is the amount for which an asset could be exchanged, or a liability settled, between knowledgeable, willing parties in an arm's length transaction.

Illustration

On 1 April 2006 an 8% convertible loan note with a nominal value of $600,000 was issued at par. It is redeemable on 31 March 2010 also at par. Alternatively it may be converted into equity shares of Question Inc on the basis of 100 new shares for each $200 of loan note.

An equivalent loan note **without** the conversion option would have carried interest at 10%. Interest of $48,000 has already been paid and included as a finance cost.

Present value rates are as follows:

End of Year	Present Values 8%	10%
1	0.93	0.91
2	0.86	0.83
3	0.79	0.75
4	0.73	0.68

We are required to show the treatment of the above loan notes in the financial statements for the year ended 31 March 2007.

We approach this by looking at the 'substance' of the loan note initially. We can see that there is an 'option' to convert the shares into equity i.e. the loan note holders do not have to accept equity shares; they could demand repayment in the form of cash. So is it a debt instrument or an equity instrument? We look to the provisions of IAS 32 'Financial Instruments: Presentation' for the correct treatment.

Step 1

IAS 32 states that where there is an obligation to transfer economic benefits there should be a liability recognised. On the other hand, where there is **not** an obligation to transfer economic benefits, a financial instrument should be recognised as equity.

In the facts above, we have both – 'equity' *and* 'debt' (i.e. a 'compound' financial instrument). There is an obligation to pay cash – i.e. interest at 8% per annum and a redemption amount – this is our 'debt'. The 'equity' part of the transaction is the option to convert.

Now we have deciphered that the financial instrument is a 'mix' of debt and equity (a compound financial instrument), we need to consider how to recognise this in the statement of financial position and the statement of comprehensive income.

Step 2

The question gives us present value rates and these need to be used to calculate the 'debt' element of the financial instrument so as to recognise the liability at its *present value* (note – what is worth $100 now won't be worth $100 in 5 years time), hence 'discounting' to present day values. But what rate do we use? 8% - because that's the value of the interest payable on the loan note???

No.

We have been told in the question that an *equivalent* loan note *without* the conversion option would have carried interest at **10%** - this is the value we use to discount the future cash flows. But what cash flows?

Going back to the question we have been told that $48,000 has been paid as interest ($600,000 x 8%). The loan note is redeemed on 31 March 2010, so we can calculate the 'debt' element of the loan note as follows:

	8% Interest ($600,000 x 8%)	Factor at a rate of 10%	PV
Year 1 2007	48,000	0.91	43,600
Year 2 2008	48,000	0.83	39,800
Year 3 2009	48,000	0.75	36,000
			119,400
Year 4 * 2010	648,000	0.68	440,600
Amount to be recognised as a liability			560,000
Initial proceeds			(600,000)
Amount to be recognised as equity			40,000

*In year 4 the loan note is redeemed therefore $600,000 + $48,000 = $648,000.

Step 3

The next thing we have to look at is the interest charge that we have already charged to the income statement. The question states that $48,000 has been recognised in the statement of comprehensive income i.e. $600,000 x 8% - but that's not the end of the answer!

The 8% loan note is simply the interest the loan note holders receive annually. We have to recognise that an *equivalent* loan *without* the conversion option would carry interest at a higher rate i.e. 10%, so it is therefore necessary to reflect this. It would be inappropriate to show a liability discounted at 10% with a finance cost of 8%!

Another way to look at it is that we have discounted the present value of future interest payments and redemption amount using discount factors of 10%, so the finance cost charge in the statement of comprehensive income must also be recognised at the same rate i.e. for the purposes of consistency, therefore the finance cost charged to the income statement should also represent a rate of 10%. So, the present value of the 'debt' component (liability) of the financial instrument is $560,000. The finance cost at 10% is ($560,000 x 10%) $56,000, but we have already charged $48,000 (per the question), so we need to accrue a further ($56,000 - $48,000) $8,000, which needs to be added to the financial instrument as follows:

Dr Statement of comp income (finance costs)   8,000
Cr liability   8,000

Being additional interest charge on the financial instrument.

Derivatives

A derivative is a financial instrument:

- whose value changes in response to a change in underlying variables e.g. interest rates;
- that requires no initial investment, or one that is smaller than would be required for a contract with a similar response to changes in market factors; and
- is settled at a future date.

Examples of derivatives are:

- forward contracts;
- swaps;
- forward rate agreements;
- options; and

- caps and floors.

Embedded Derivatives

An embedded derivative is a feature within a contract. It acts as a component part of a 'hybrid' financial instrument which also includes a non-derivative host contract with the effect that some of the cash flows of the hybrid instrument vary in a similar way to a stand-alone derivative. A 'hybrid' instrument is a combination of both the host contract and the embedded derivative.

Embedded derivatives can arise from deliberate financial engineering (e.g. to make a low interest rate debt more attractive by including an equity-linked return). This situation is not absolute and they can arise through market prices and other contractual arrangements – for example leases and insurance contracts. In fact they can occur in all sorts of contracts and instruments with the objective being to change the nature of cash flows that would otherwise be required by the host contract and effectively shift financial risks between the parties.

Illustration

Astra Inc has a loan that pays interest based on changes in the FTSE index.

The component of the contract that is to repay the principal amount is the 'host' contract (this is the 'base state' with a predetermined term and predetermined cash flows).

The component that is to pay interest based on the FTSE index is the embedded derivative. This component causes some (or all) of the cash flows of the host contract.

Derecognition of a Financial Instrument

Financial Liabilities

A financial liability should be removed from the statement of financial position (balance sheet) when, and only when, the obligation specified within the contract is discharged, cancelled or expired. A gain or loss arising on the derecognition of a financial liability is recognised in the statement of comprehensive income (income statement).

Financial Assets

Financial assets require a bit more analysis. An entity needs to consider whether the asset under consideration is:

- an asset in its entirety; or
- specifically identified cash flows from an asset; or
- a fully proportionate share of the cash flows from an asset; or
- a fully proportionate share of specifically identified cash flows from a financial asset.

Once this has been undertaken consideration is then given to whether the asset has been transferred, and if so, whether the transfer of the asset is eligible for derecognition. An asset is transferred if either the entity has transferred the contractual rights to receive cash flows, or the entity has retained the contractual rights to receive the cash flows from the asset, but has assumed a contractual obligation to pass those cash flows on under an arrangement which meets three conditions:

- the entity does not pay the amounts over until it collects an equivalent amount on the original asset;
- the entity is prohibited from selling or pledging the original asset other than to the recipient; and
- the entity has an obligation to remit those funds to the recipient without delay.

The key factor is looking at whether all the risks and rewards have also been transferred. If substantially all of the risks and rewards of ownership have been passed, then the entity can derecognise the asset. If substantially all of the risks and rewards have not been passed over, then the entity is prohibited from derecognising the asset.

Subsequent Measurement of Financial Assets and Financial Liabilities

	In Statement of Financial Position	Gains or Losses
Fair value through profit or loss	Fair value	Statement of Comprehensive Income
Available for sale	Fair value	In equity until derecognition, then recycled via the statement of comprehensive income.
Held-to-maturity	At amortised cost	Not applicable
Loans and receivables	At amortised cost	Not applicable

Hedge Accounting

In order to qualify for hedge accounting at the inception of a hedge and at each reporting date, the changes in the fair value or cash flows of the hedged item attributable to the hedged risk must be expected to be highly effective in offsetting the changes in the fair value or the cash flows of the hedging instrument on a prospective basis and on a retrospective basis where the actual results are within a range of 80% to 125% when offset by an opposite gain or loss.

Categories

There are three types of hedge:

- fair value hedge;
- cash flow hedge; and
- hedge of a net investment in a foreign operation

For hedge accounting to be applied, certain criteria must be met:

- there must be formal document put in place at the inception of the hedge;
- the designation between the item that is hedged and the hedging instrument itself is formally documented;
- hedge effectiveness can be measured;
- where cash flow hedges are concerned, the transaction must be highly probable (i.e. more likely than not); and
- assessment takes place on an on-going basis and is effective throughout the period.

Fair Value Hedge
A fair value hedge is a hedge of the exposure to changes in the fair value of a recognised asset or liability or a firm commitment that is attributable to a particular risk which could affect profit or loss.

The gain or loss from remeasuring the hedging instrument at fair value (for a derivative hedging instrument) or foreign currency component measured in accordance with IAS 21, is recognised in profit or loss.

The gain or loss on the hedged item attributable to the hedged risk will adjust the carrying amount of the hedged item and should be recognised in profit or loss even if the hedged item is measured at cost. Recognition in profit or loss also applies if the hedged item is an available-for-sale financial asset.

Cash Flow Hedge
A cash flow hedge is a hedge against the exposure to variability in cash flows associated with a recognised asset or liability which could affect profit or loss.

The portion of the gain or loss on the hedging instrument that is determined to be an effective hedge is recognised in other comprehensive income.

The ineffective portion of the gain or loss on the hedging instrument is recognised in profit or loss.

Hedge of a Net Investment in a Foreign Operation

Is linked to IAS 21 and is a foreign operation (i.e. a subsidiary). The portion of the gain or loss on the hedging instrument that is determined to be an effective hedge is recognised in other comprehensive income.

The ineffective portion is recognised in profit or loss.

IAS 40
Investment Property

OBJECTIVE

The objective of this standard is to prescribe the accounting treatment that an entity should apply in dealing with its investment property.

Investment Property

Investment property is property held for its investment potential. Investment property, therefore is not property for:

- use in the production of supply of goods or services or for administrative purposes; or
- sale in the ordinary course of business.

Recognition

Investment property must be recognised as an asset when, and only when:

- it is probable that the future economic benefits that are associated with the investment property will flow to the entity; and
- the cost of the investment property can be measured reliably.

An investment property should initially be recorded at its cost.

Subsequent Measurement

IAS 40 allows investment property to be subsequently measured using either the:

- cost model; or
- fair value model.

The cost model is that used in IAS 16 and requires an investment property to be measured at depreciated cost after initial recognition. Where an entity chooses this model for subsequent measurement it must disclose the fair value of its investment property within the financial statements.

IAS 41
Agriculture

OBJECTIVE

The objective of this standard is to prescribe the accounting treatment related to agricultural activity.

Agricultural Activity

Agricultural activity is the management by an entity of the biological transformation of biological assets for sale into agricultural produce or additional biological assets.

Biological Asset

A biological asset is a living animal or plant.

Agricultural Produce

Agricultural produce is the harvested product of an entity's biological asset.

Initial Measurement

Biological assets should be measured initially, and at each reporting date, at fair value less estimated point-of-sale costs.

Agricultural produce is measured at the point of harvest at fair value less estimated point-of-sale costs

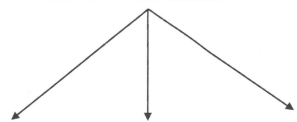

Point of Sale Costs include:

Commissions to brokers/dealers   levies by regulatory bodies   transfer taxes/duties

They do not, however, include costs such as transport or other such costs needed to get the asset to market.

Fair Value

There is a rebuttable presumption within IAS 41 that says the presumption can be rebutted on initial recognition when market prices are not available and alternative estimates of fair value are clearly unreliable. Where this occurs, an entity should value its biological assets at cost less accumulated depreciation and any impairment losses.

IAS 41 requires that a change in fair value less estimated point-of-sale costs of a biological asset be included in net profit or loss for the period in which it arises. In agricultural activity, a change in physical attributes of a living plant or animal directly enhances or diminishes economic benefits to the entity.

Illustration

Biological Asset	Agricultural Produce	Harvested Product
Cattle	Milk	Cheese
Bushes	Leaf	Tea, tobacco
Vines	Grape	Wine
Plants	Cotton	Thread, clothing
Sheep	Wool	Yarn

Government Grants

If a government grant related to a biological asset measured at its fair value less estimated point-of-sale costs is conditional, including where a government grant requires an enterprise not to engage in specified agricultural activity, an enterprise should recognise the government grant as income when, and only when, the conditions attaching to the grant are met.

If a government grant relates to a biological asset measured at cost less depreciation and impairment, then the provisions in IAS 20 apply.

Illustration

On 1 January 2007 Farmer Smith held a herd of ten 2 year old animals. He purchased an animal aged 2.5 years on 1 July 2007 for $108 and one animal was born on 1 July 2007. No animals were sold or disposed of during the period. Per-unit fair values less estimated point-of-sale costs were as follows:

	$	
2 year old animal at 1 January 2007	100	
Newborn animal at 1 July 2007	70	
2.5 year old animal at 1 July 2007	108	
Newborn animal at 31 December 2007	72	
0.5 year old animal at 31 December 2007	80	
2 year old animal at 31 December 2007	105	
2.5 year old animal at 31 December 2007	111	
3 year old animal at 31 December 2007	120	

Fair value less estimated point-of-sale costs of herd:

At 1 January 2007   (10 x $100)   1,000

Purchase 1 July 2007   (1 x $108)   108

Increase in fair value less estimated point-of-sale costs due to price change:

10 x ($105 – $100)   50

1 x ($111- $108)   3

1 x ($72 - $70)   2   55

Increase in fair value less estimated point-of-sale costs due to physical change:

10 x ($120 - $105)   150

1 x ($120 - $111)   9

1 x ($80 - $72)   8

1 x $70   70   237

Fair value less estimated point-of-sale costs of herd:

at 31 December 2007

11 x $120   1,320

1 x $80   80   1,400

International Accounting Standards are fast becoming a global feature with more countries switching from domestic standards to International. Most of the international standards are complex and technical. This book aims to summarise the core technical aspects of the accounting standards in an easy to understand format.

Most chapters contain illustrative examples of how the standard works in practice as well as defining some of the more complex and technical terms users often come across when reporting under IFRS.

authorHOUSE®

ISBN 978-1-4389-9319-5

90000

9 781438 993195